TARTS

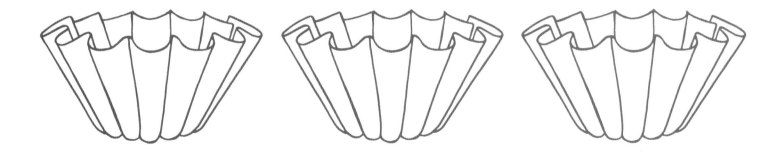

First published in Great Britain by Simon & Schuster UK Ltd, 2003
A Viacom Company

Simon & Schuster UK Ltd
Africa House
64–78 Kingsway
London
WC2B 6AH

1 3 5 7 9 10 8 6 4 2

Design: **Fiona Andreanelli**
Typesetting: **Stylize Digital Artwork**
Food photography: **Steve Baxter**
Home economist: **David Morgan**
Stylist for food photography: **Liz Belton**
Editor: **Paula Borton**
Printed and bound in China

ISBN 0 74324 010 3

Best-kept Secrets of the Women's Institute

TARTS

Liz Herbert

SIMON & SCHUSTER
A VIACOM COMPANY

ACKNOWLEDGEMENTS

I would like to dedicate this book to the well-known cookery writer Sonia Allison, who sadly passed away during the compilation of this book. Sonia made it possible for me, as a newly qualified home economist, to obtain a start in cookery writing. She opened my eyes to the limitless possibilities of recipe creation, with her drive and enthusiasm.

Writing this book has introduced our three-year-old twins to 'paystrie', as an alternative to play dough. Our eldest, Susie, has been a great morale booster – my greatest fan, and James is my number one food critic.

My gratitude go to family and friends who have sampled the recipes and given supportive feedback. Also thanks to my husband, Nigel, for his computer skills and for paying the price of intense recipe testing with extra visits to the gym!

CONTENTS

INTRODUCTION

The first thing I do when I pick up a cookery book is to look at the photographs, and if they say, '**eat me**', then, I'll read the recipe. So I have to thank all those involved in the food photography and design layout of this book that you have got this far!

When I was first approached to write this book in the Best-kept Secrets of the Women's Institute series, I was delighted with the scope that such a title offers – tarts as appetisers, starters garnished with a salad or piquant salsa, traditional desserts or a *piéce de résistance*, the triumphant finale to round off an enjoyable meal. The more recipes that I created the more drawn I became to the whole concept of pastry making. As a heavy-handed dough maker (my second job was at a company which promoted the national sales of bread and flour), I was able to produce tarts which looked the part, but I cannot pretend they had a 'melt-in-the-mouth' texture. However, thanks to my trusty food processor and the addition of an increased fat to flour ratio, my pastry making has improved – hope for any other faint-hearted pastry makers out there!

There is something about serving a home made tart that goes way beyond the boundaries of filling a hole – hunger is only one of the criteria. There is the satisfaction of producing, from scratch, a unique creation – no two tarts will look identical, or taste exactly the same. Together with this is the time which has been devoted to its making, that ultimately manifests itself as an act of love. Sadly these connotations have been lost on my family, who, it has to be said, may well have suffered from over exposure!

This book has been divided into sections based on traditional, contemporary and the influence of Continental tarts, with an initial chapter devoted to appetisers. I hope that I have achieved a balance. There are the classic timeless tarts – such as Quiche Lorraine (page 25), Pissaladière (page 21), Lemon Meringue Pie (page 39) and Bakewell Tart (page 40) – that have earned themselves a place in our heritage, and as such, to be passed down from generation to generation. While at the other end of the spectrum, I have incorporated some more modern ideas – Garlic Mushroom and Taleggio Tart (page 35), Rhubarb and White Chocolate Flan (page 73) and Baked Nectarine and Blueberry Tart (page 76). These make use of the increasingly wide range of produce on offer, dairy products in particular, and bought pastry, of course, reflecting today's trend for quick recipes, while not compromising on taste.

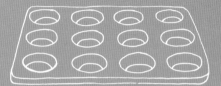 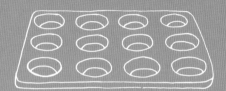 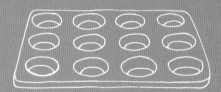

As a final note, do remember that one of the joys of having a range of pastry types is the flexibility this affords. Although I have recommended a certain type of pastry for each recipe, in many cases they are interchangeable, allowing you to influence your final dish by choosing your particular preference.

Whether you have bought this book for yourself, or have been given it as a present, I hope that you will be inspired by the recipes and delighted with your results.

PASTRY-MAKING PRINCIPLES

Any form of cookery requires some basic skills, which, once mastered become second nature. Pastry-making probably needs more know-how than others, in that there are different types of pastry, with quite contrasting textures, ratio of ingredients and desired appearance. Even if you prefer to use ready-made fresh or frozen pastry, it is as well to understand the principles of pastry-making in order to achieve the best results.

The golden rule of pastry-making is to keep everything as cool as you possibly can. In the days when I was learning how to cook it was suggested that a marble slab, and even a marble rolling pin, were essential for perfect pastry. All well and good if you have them, but I would not rush out and buy them if not! On a more scientific level, things should be kept as cold as possible in order to help separate the gluten in the flour from the fat, which will result in a shorter, crumblier pastry.

There are several ways in which you can ensure that everything is kept as cool as possible:
- Do not work under bright kitchen lights – modern halogen ones in particular emit a lot of heat.
- Make sure that your fat is cut into small cubes (this makes rubbing in quicker).
- Take your fat straight from the fridge (or even the freezer during the summer).
- Measure out the water beforehand and put in the fridge to cool.
- DO NOT SKIP THE CHILLING STAGE. This is very important, otherwise the pastry case will shrink back during cooking, causing the filling to overflow and ooze out in a flood all over the oven.

PASTRY POINTERS

Fat: It is the fat in pastry, which gives it flavour and affects the crumb – making it short and light. Generally, block margarine can be substituted for butter, and lard and vegetable shortening are interchangeable.

Water: Makes pastry crumbly but it also has the effect of causing the pastry to shrink during cooking as it evaporates in the heat. Egg yolk or whole egg is therefore sometimes used instead.

Handling: It is important to try not to handle the pastry more than is absolutely necessary, and to treat it very gently. This is because if you overwork the dough you will be developing the gluten in it, and it is this that causes the pastry to toughen. You may notice this if the pastry springs back when you are rolling out. Use plain flour as this has a lower gluten content than strong bread flour.

Rolling Out: You will need to use a little flour to prevent the dough from sticking to the work surface and rolling pin, but you need to be careful not to use too much as this will change the consistency of the pastry. Therefore lightly sprinkle a little over the work surface and rolling pin, but not the pastry itself. Remembering that pastry-making requires a light touch, use gentle, even strokes, rolling in one direction only – away from your body. Avoid stretching the dough and rotate the pastry a quarter turn after each roll, to maintain an even circular shape. Stop your rolling pin at the edge of the pastry, do not roll it off the work surface, this way you will keep a uniform thickness. It helps if the pastry is at the correct temperature when rolling out: too warm and the fat becomes oily, resulting in a sticky dough; too cold and it tends to crack and be stiff to roll.

Lining Flan Tin: Generally the tin will not need greasing. Roll out the pastry to roughly 5 cm (2 inches) larger than the tin. Carefully wrap the pastry around the rolling pin, lift and unroll over the tin, easing it gently into the bottom edges, being careful to avoid stretching it, as it will just shrink during cooking. This will also press out any trapped air. To remove any excess pastry, roll the rolling pin over the top (the sharp edges will act as a knife), again turning the tin, so that you are always rolling away from you. Then, carefully, with the back of your bent forefinger, smooth the pastry slightly so that it stands just proud of the rim.

Pricking: Puncturing the base of the pastry with a fork releases any trapped air, thus preventing the pastry from rising up during cooking.

Chilling: The pastry needs to rest, in order for the gluten to 'shrink' back. This avoids the pastry collapsing down the sides of the tin during baking, leaving you with a shallow shell with spilt filling. There are two stages at which this can be done, and for rich pastries you may wish to do so at both opportunities. Firstly, after the dough has been made, it may be refrigerated for 30–60 minutes. It is important to wrap it in a plastic bag or clingfilm to prevent it drying out, as it will then crack when you come to roll it out. Alternatively, line your flan ring once you have made the dough, prick the base, and then refrigerate, for 30–60 minutes. The pastry will not need covering unless you plan to leave it overnight.

Baking Blind: This literally means baking the pastry shell without the filling inside. The shell can be either partially cooked, if a filling which requires baking is to be added, or completely cooked for a cold filling, such as for fruit and custard flans, or canapé savouries. By baking blind you prevent the pastry underneath from becoming soggy. To bake blind: lay a round of foil or greaseproof paper over the uncooked pastry, half fill the tin with baking beans, macaroni, dried beans or rice, to weigh it down. Bake in the centre of a preheated oven, on a metal baking tray, for 15 minutes. Remove beans and paper and bake for a further 5–15 minutes, depending on whether any further cooking is required.

Tins: Generally a metal, loose-bottomed flan tin is ideal for pastry-making. The removable base means that the tart can be eased out of the tin to serve, which looks attractive, and, because metal is a good conductor of heat, the pastry cooks through. Porcelain and ceramic dishes do look attractive, but you will probably not achieve such crisp pastry. For this same reason, I always recommend placing the flan tin on a baking sheet to cook. The size of the tin stated, actually refers to the measurement of the diameter of the bottom, which can quite often be smaller than the top!

Storing: Unfilled pastry dough freezes well. Bought pastry can either be purchased fresh or frozen. However, the filling will dictate whether or not the tart is suitable for freezing. On the whole, tarts are best eaten fresh, or, if they have been frozen, should be heated through in the oven, to crisp them up before serving. Shortcrust, puff and filo should be wrapped and stored in the fridge for three days, or may be frozen for up to three months.

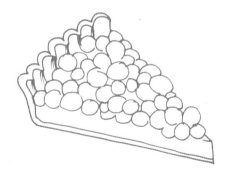

Bought Pastry: My recipes state a size of tin, lined with pastry made using a quantity of flour. If using bought pastry you will need to buy double the weight, i.e. for a flan case made with 115 g (4 oz) flour you will need to purchase a 225 g (8 oz) packet.

Machine Mixers: Mixers and processors are excellent for pastry making, in that no warmth is involved because there is no need for you to use your hands. However, you do have to be very careful not to over mix as this will strengthen the gluten, making the pastry tough, and very hard to handle as it will shrink back. It is vital to stop the machine as soon as the mixture has come together into a pastry dough. If in doubt, stop the machine before this stage and bring it together by hand on a lightly floured work surface.

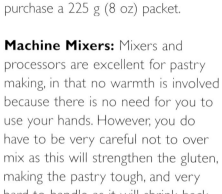

BASIC SHORTCRUST PASTRY

Shortcrust pastry is probably the most widely used pastry, and certainly the first to master if you are new to pastry-making. It is a soft, manageable dough, which can be filled for tarts and used also for pies. Bought shortcrust, fresh or frozen, is readily available. If substituting this for the quantities in a recipe, you will need double the quantity of bought to home made – so if a recipe uses 115 g (4 oz) plain flour you will need 225 g (8 oz) bought shortcrust.

115 g (4 oz) plain flour
25 g (1 oz) butter or block margarine
25 g (1 oz) lard or white vegetable fat
30 ml (2 tablespoons) cold water

1   Place the flour in a bowl.
2   Cut the fats into small pieces, and using just the tips of your fingers, and lifting the flour up as you work (so as to incorporate air into the pastry), rub them into the flour. The mixture should resemble fine breadcrumbs.
3   Sprinkle water over the surface and, using a round bladed knife, mix. The dough will look lumpy and should be soft but not sticky.
4   Turn out on to a lightly floured work surface and gently form into a soft, flattened ball, ready for rolling.

Using a food processor: Place all ingredients, except the water, in the bowl and pulse until the mixture resembles fine breadcrumbs. Turn the motor on again and add the water through the funnel. As soon as the dough comes together in a ball stop the machine. Turn the dough out on to a lightly floured surface and proceed from step 4.

This quantity is sufficient to line a shallow 23 cm (9-inch) or a deep 20 cm (8-inch) flan tin. Shortcrust pastry is usually cooked at Gas Mark 6/electric oven 200°C/fan oven 180°C.

SWEET RICH SHORTCRUST

This is my favourite pastry. It is very easy to make in a food processor, handles well and results in a lovely rich, short crumb. The following quantity is sufficient for a shallow 23 cm (9-inch) tart tin, or a deep 20 cm (8-inch) tin. Pastries flavoured with sugar are cooked at a lower temperature to prevent the sugar from burning. Bake at Gas Mark 5/electric oven 190°C/fan oven 170°C.

115 g (4 oz) plain flour
80 g (3 oz) unsalted butter
2 tablespoons icing sugar
1 egg yolk

1   Place the flour, butter and icing sugar in a processor. Turn on and blend until the mixture resembles fine breadcrumbs.
2   With the motor running add the egg yolk through the funnel, and process until the dough comes together.
3   Turn out on to a floured surface and gently bring together using your fingertips.

PÂTE SUCRÉE

This is a traditional French, almost biscuit-like pastry – the one classically used for Continental tarts. It is rich and quite tricky to handle. This pastry is made on the worktop (marble slab if possible) and does need to be chilled for at least 1 hour before using. Nowadays I make it in a food processor, substituting 15 ml (1 tablespoon) of water for one of the egg yolks. Follow the same method as for ordinary shortcrust. This quantity is sufficient to line a shallow 23 cm (9-inch) or deep 20 cm (8 inch) flan tin, and is usually baked at Gas Mark 5/electric oven 190°C/fan oven 170°C.

115 g (4 oz) plain flour
a pinch of salt
50 g (2 oz) unsalted butter, softened
50 g (2 oz) caster sugar
2 egg yolks

1 Sift the flour and salt on to a work surface. Make a well in the centre.
2 Put butter, sugar and egg yolks into the middle of the flour.
3 Using one hand, work the butter, sugar and egg yolks together, until thoroughly mixed.
4 Then gradually incorporate the flour, bringing in a little at a time, until it is all worked in and you have a very soft dough.
5 Wrap the pastry in clingfilm or a plastic bag and chill in the fridge for at least 1 hour.

FILO PASTRY

I always buy filo pastry, either fresh or frozen, as the results are excellent and it saves so much time. However, it is tricky when writing a recipe, because different companies produce their sheets in varying sizes. So it is really a matter of sticking to one brand, or just having slightly different dimensions for your dish.

Filo is the name given to this pastry in the Middle East, and strudel is the European counterpart, they are exactly the same pastry.

Filo pastry is so thin that you can almost trace a pattern through it, and for this reason needs careful handling as it is very brittle, and prone to drying out. Any pastry that you are not working with at the time should be wrapped in a damp tea towel, or plastic bag. Its very low fat content means that it is necessary to add butter when using, with the added advantage that it renders it moist, making the sheets pliable and enabling them to be held together.

Serving tarts as a starter or as appetisers with drinks has, to my mind, two very great advantages: firstly, most tarts are best eaten warm – which allows for a little lee-way while guests arrive and secondly, they can be prepared in advance as they reheat extremely well.

APPETISERS & STARTERS

These small tarts are guaranteed to tantalize the palate, whetting the appetite for the courses to follow. You could also try scaling down some of the savoury tarts in other chapters if you like.

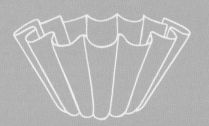  

SERVES 6
PREPARATION & COOKING TIME:
15 minutes + 50–60 minutes cooking
FREEZING: not recommended

If you have not tried tapenade before I'm sure that this recipe will convert you. Its concentrated flavour means that a little goes a long way. Varieties based on red pepper and black or green olives are available in most major supermarkets. If you are not keen on feta you can use marinated artichoke hearts instead (also available in supermarkets). To make these tartlets into appetisers to hand round with drinks, cut each of them into six slices. Alternatively add some tuna chunks or Italian salami to make a more substantial lunch dish.

TOMATO TAPENADE TARTLETS

FOR THE PASTRY:
500 g packet puff pastry

FOR THE FILLING:
2 red peppers
2 tablespoons black olive tapenade
175 g (6 oz) feta cheese, diced
115 g (4 oz) cherry tomatoes, quartered
scant 25 g (1 oz) pine kernels
basil leaves
extra virgin olive oil, for brushing

1 Preheat the oven as high as it will go. Place the red peppers in a roasting dish and cook for 35–40 minutes until they are charred. Remove them from the oven immediately and place them in a polythene bag. Secure the bag and allow the peppers to cool – this helps the skins to peel off easily.

2 Reduce the oven temperature to Gas Mark 7/electric oven 220°C/fan oven 200°C.

3 On a lightly floured surface roll out the pastry and, using a plate as a guide, cut out six 13 cm (5-inch) rounds. Place the pastry on two baking sheets. Score a line on each round 1 cm (½ inch) in from the edge.

4 Spread 1 teaspoon of tapenade on top of each round and, using a palette knife, smooth it over the surface as far as the scored rim.

5 Dot feta cheese over the top of each tart and then add the tomatoes.

6 Remove the peppers from the bag, discard the skin and seeds, and slice them. Arrange the pepper slices over the tarts.

7 Sprinkle with pine kernels and scatter a few basil leaves over each – brush these with olive oil to prevent them from burning.

8 Bake the tartlets towards the top of the oven for 15–20 minutes, until the pastry is puffy and golden.

MAKES 12
PREPARATION & COOKING TIME:
25 minutes + 25–30 minutes cooking
FREEZING: not recommended

These **moreish** little tartlets make ideal summer appetisers. A simple green salad with plenty of watercress or rocket would set these off superbly.

1 garlic clove, peeled
¼ teaspoon sea salt
1 tablespoon olive oil
4 medium tomatoes, skinned, de-seeded and chopped
1 small red chilli, de-seeded and chopped finely
a pinch of sugar
115 g (4 oz) fresh, peeled prawns
2 sheets 48 cm x 26 cm (19 inches x 10½ inches) filo pastry
40 g (1½ oz) butter, melted
80 g (3 oz) mozzarella cheese, cut into small cubes
50 g (2 oz) breadcrumbs
1 tablespoon chopped fresh parsley
freshly ground black pepper

1 Preheat the oven to Gas Mark 5/electric oven 190°C/fan oven 170°C.
2 Crush the garlic and salt together in a pestle and mortar to make a smooth purée. Heat the oil in a frying-pan. Sauté the garlic with the tomatoes and chopped chilli for 8–10 minutes, until the mixture is reduced to a pulp. Season with pepper and a pinch of sugar. Stir in the prawns.
3 Lay the sheets of filo on the work surface, one on top of the other, making sure the edges match exactly. Arrange the pastry so that the shortest edge is at the top. Cut it from top to bottom into three equal strips. Now cut it in half across the centre. You should have six pieces. Stack these on top of each other and cut across twice to make three equal squares. Take a 12-hole patty tin. You will need three squares of pastry for each hole. Take one square and brush it with melted butter and place it in the patty tin. Do the same with a second square, but lay it at an angle over the first. Repeat with a third square, so that you have a sort of star effect. Repeat with the remaining filo to make 12 tartlets
5 Bake these in the oven for 6–8 minutes, or until just golden.
6 Spoon the prawn and tomato mixture into the pastry cases. Scatter cubes of mozzarella cheese over each one.
7 Stir the breadcrumbs into the remaining melted butter and add the parsley. Sprinkle this over the top of tarts. Bake the tartlets in the oven for 15–20 minutes, until the breadcrumbs are crisp and golden and the cheese is melted. Serve at once.

NOTE: Never reheat a dish containing prawns.

PRAWN, FRESH TOMATO & MOZZARELLA TARTLETS

MAKES 12
PREPARATION & COOKING TIME:
25 minutes + 15–20 minutes cooking
FREEZING: recommended

CHICKEN FILO TARTLETS

These tartlets make a delicious starter. I have also cooked them in mini muffin trays to make tasty appetisers to hand round with drinks. Don't be put off by the length of the instructions for preparing the tartlet cases; it really is quite straightforward! To prepare these in advance, you can bake the pastry cases and then cook the filling separately. Just prior to serving, fill the cases and pop them into the oven at Gas Mark 4/electric oven 180°C/fan oven 160°C for 15–20 minutes to warm through and crisp up.

FOR THE PASTRY:
2 sheets 48 cm x 26 cm (19 inches x 10½ inches) filo pastry
25 g (1 oz) butter, melted

FOR THE FILLING:
2 tablespoons olive oil
4 plum tomatoes, skinned and chopped roughly
1 garlic clove, peeled
¼ teaspoon sea salt
350 g (12 oz) chicken breasts, chopped small
6 sun dried tomatoes chopped finely
small amount of fresh chilli paste, to taste
150 ml (5 fl oz) double cream
freshly ground black pepper

1 Preheat the oven to Gas Mark 5/electric oven 190°C/fan oven 170°C. Lay one sheet of filo pastry on the work surface and place the other exactly on top, making sure the edges meet. Arrange the pastry so that the shortest edge is at the top.

2 Cut the pastry from top to bottom into three equal strips. Now cut the strips in half across the centre. You should have six pieces. Stack these pieces on top of each other and cut across twice to make three equal squares.

3 Take a 12-hole patty tin. You will need three squares of pastry for each hole. Take one square and brush it with melted butter and place it in the patty tin. Do the same with a second square, but lay it at an angle over the first. Repeat with a third square, so that you have a sort of star effect. Repeat with the remaining filo to make 12 tartlets

4 Bake in the centre of the oven for just 6–8 minutes, checking regularly to make sure that they end up golden, but not burnt!

5 Meanwhile, prepare the filling. Heat the oil and add the chopped tomatoes. Crush the garlic and salt together in a pestle and mortar, to a smooth purée and add it to the tomato mixture. Cook for about 5 minutes, until the tomatoes are soft.

6 Add the chopped chicken breasts, sun dried tomatoes and chilli paste. Cook for 2–3 minutes, until the chicken turns opaque.

7 Stir in the cream and cook briskly over a high heat, until the sauce has reduced and the chicken is tender. Season with black pepper.

8 Spoon the chicken mixture into the baked pastry cases and serve at once.

MAKES 18
PREPARATION & COOKING TIME:
25 minutes + 15–20 minutes cooking
FREEZING: recommended

LITTLE LEEK TARTS

I often find recipes that use a few, simple ingredients work best, and this is certainly one of them! The spring onions here intensify the flavour of the leeks. These tarts will freeze well if you have any left over.

FOR THE PASTRY:
425 g (15 oz) ready-made puff pastry

FOR THE FILLING:
25 g (1 oz) butter
675 g (1 lb 8 oz) leeks, chopped finely
a bunch of spring onions, chopped finely
3 tablespoons crème fraîche
1 large egg, beaten
freshly grated nutmeg
40 g (1½ oz) Cheddar cheese, grated
salt and freshly ground pepper

1 Preheat the oven to Gas Mark 7/electric oven 220°C/ fan oven 200°C.
2 Melt the butter in a large saucepan. Add the leeks and cook, covered, over a fairly low heat for 10–15 minutes without browning. They should look soft and slightly pulpy, and any excess liquid should have evaporated. Stir in the spring onions and cool the mixture slightly.
3 On a lightly floured surface roll out the pastry into a thin sheet (you will need to cut 18 circles). Using an 8 cm (3-inch) round cutter, stamp out the circles. Use them to line two patty tins. Prick the bases well with a fork.
4 Beat the crème fraîche and egg into the leek mixture. Season to taste with nutmeg and salt and pepper. Put a tablespoon of the mixture in each tart.
5 Sprinkle each with a little grated cheese and bake, just above the middle of the oven, for 15–20 minutes, or until the pastry is puffy and golden.

MAKES 6
PREPARATION & COOKING TIME:
20 minutes + 1 hour 20 minutes cooking
FREEZING: recommended

These individual tarts make a stunning starter. St. Agur cheese has a **distinctive strong flavour**, which contrasts vividly with the sweet shallots. However, you can substitute a milder blue cheese, such as gorgonzola, if you prefer. The tarts can be fully prepared in advance and just popped into the oven, ready to be served warm, when your guests arrive.

FOR THE PASTRY:
225 g (8 oz) ready-made puff pastry

FOR THE FILLING:
350 g (12 oz) shallots
25 g (1 oz) butter
1 tablespoon caster sugar
15 ml (1 tablespoon) cider vinegar
125 g packet of St. Agur cheese
1 teaspoon chopped fresh thyme
freshly ground black pepper

1   Preheat the oven to Gas Mark 7/electric oven 220°C/fan oven 200°C.
2   To peel the shallots; place them in a bowl and pour over boiling water. Leave them to stand for 2 minutes. Drain and skin. If they are large, cut them in half from top to bottom.
3   Heat the butter in a large saucepan. Sprinkle over the sugar and vinegar. Add the shallots and season well with black pepper (the cheese is very salty, so you don't need any here). Cook over a medium heat for 1 hour, turning the onions frequently until they are transparent and golden. Cool slightly.
4   On a lightly floured surface, roll out the pastry and cut out six 10 cm (4-inch) circles. Space the circles out on a baking sheet. Using a sharp knife, score a ring 1 cm (½ inch) from the edge. Now prick inside the ring all over with a fork.
5   Divide the cheese into six portions. Spread a portion over each tart, being careful not to go over the scored ring. Place the caramelised shallots on top of each tart and sprinkle with fresh thyme. Bake just above the middle of the oven, for 15–20 minutes, until the tarts are puffy and golden.

CARAMELISED SHALLOT & BLUE CHEESE TARTS

The recipes included in this chapter are a mouthwatering mix of Continental favourites, such as Pissaladière, Quiche Lorraine and Greek Spinach Filo Tart, as well as classic British fare which make use of such basic ingredients as potato, Cheddar cheese and eggs. The wholesome and filling Great English Breakfast Quiche and Farmhouse Potato Pie speak for themselves.

CLASSIC FLANS & QUICHES

The flans and quiches in this chapter really prove the versatility of tarts, with all sorts of ingredients and flavours combining to make delicious and attractive fillings. The advantage of a tart (as opposed to a pie) is that the filling is on show, so your creativity can be given full rein when it comes to presentation!

SERVES 6
PREPARATION & COOKING TIME:
30 minutes + 1½ hours proving
+ 20–25 minutes cooking
FREEZING: recommended

Pissaladière combines elements of quiche and pizza, unsurprisingly as it is a native dish of Provence where the cuisine is greatly influenced by neighbouring Italy. Subtle variations in the dish occur according to regions – wine, tomatoes and garlic may or may not be included. Likewise the tart may be dough or pastry based.

PISSALADIÈRE

FOR THE DOUGH:

225 g (8 oz) strong white bread flour
½ teaspoon salt
7 g sachet of easy blend dried yeast
1 tablespoon olive oil
150 ml (5 fl oz) warm water

FOR THE FILLING:

4 tablespoons olive oil, plus extra for brushing
900 g (2 lb) Spanish onions, peeled, halved and sliced thinly
1 teaspoon fresh chopped thyme, or ½ teaspoon dried thyme
2 garlic cloves, crushed
350 g (12 oz) tomatoes, skinned, de-seeded and chopped
50 g can of anchovy fillets, drained and halved lengthways
12 black olives, stoned and halved
salt and freshly ground black pepper
fresh oregano, to garnish

1　For the dough, mix together the flour, salt and yeast. Stir in the oil and water and mix to a soft dough. Turn the dough out on to a work surface and knead for 10 minutes until it feels smooth. Place in an oiled polythene bag and leave it in a warm place for about 1 hour, to double in size.

2　To make the filling, heat the oil in a large saucepan. Add the onions, thyme and garlic and sauté, covered, for 30 minutes. Stir the mixture occasionally, until it begins to soften. Remove the lid and continue cooking for a further 30 minutes until the liquid has evaporated, stirring occasionally. Season with salt and pepper. Cool the mixture slightly.

3　Preheat the oven to Gas Mark 7/electric oven 220°C/fan oven 200°C.

4　Push the dough into an oiled rectangular baking tin 28 cm x 23 cm (11 inches x 9 inches). Brush the surface with olive oil and then spread it with the onion mixture. Scatter chopped tomatoes over the top. Arrange the anchovy fillets in a diamond pattern and stud with halved olives. Prove in a warm place for 30 minutes before baking in the centre of the oven for 20–25 minutes. Serve scattered with fresh oregano leaves.

SERVES 6
PREPARATION & COOKING TIME:
40 minutes + 30 minutes cooking
FREEZING: not recommended

Semolina is a wonderful basis for pastry. The pastry case for this tart does not require baking blind and has a crisp, nutty texture. This would make a good 'all-in-one' lunch dish. Reheating dries out the fish, but you could prepare the tart in advance and then bake it just prior to serving.

FOR THE SEMOLINA PASTRY:
80 g (3 oz) semolina
80 g (3 oz) plain flour
80 g (3 oz) butter

FOR THE FILLING:
225 g (8 oz) undyed smoked
haddock fillets, skinned
300 ml (10 fl oz) creamy milk
1 bay leaf
a few parsley stalks
4 black peppercorns
25 g (1 oz) butter
1 small onion, chopped finely
25 g (1 oz) plain flour
30 ml (2 tablespoons) double cream
2 tablespoons chopped fresh parsley
2 large egg yolks, beaten
225 g (8 oz) cooked waxy potatoes, diced
115 g (4 oz) spinach, wilted and well drained
50 g (2 oz) sweetcorn kernels

1   First make the pastry. Mix together the semolina and flour. Rub in the butter and mix to a dough with 1½ tablespoons cold water. Turn out the dough on to a floured work surface and roll it out to line a 23 cm (9-inch) loose-bottomed flan tin. Prick the base well with a fork and chill for 30 minutes, while you prepare the filling.

2   Preheat the oven to Gas Mark 5/electric oven 190°C/fan oven 170°C. Place a baking sheet on the middle shelf.

3   Place the haddock in a medium saucepan with the milk, bay leaf, parsley stalks and peppercorns. Bring to the boil and simmer for 2–3 minutes, until the fish is just cooked. (It will cook further in the oven later, so you don't want to dry it out.) Remove it from the liquid and flake into large pieces (reserve the milk).

4   Melt the butter in a small saucepan and sauté the onion for about 10 minutes, without browning, until it is soft. Stir in the flour and cook for 1 minute. Strain the milk and gradually whisk it in. When the sauce boils, stir in the cream. Remove the pan from heat, add the parsley and cool slightly. Beat in the egg yolks.

5   Scatter the diced, cooked potatoes over the pastry base. Dot the wilted spinach evenly over the top. Add the sweetcorn and haddock and then pour over the sauce. Bake (on the warmed baking sheet) immediately for about 30 minutes, or until the pastry is golden and the filling is set.

HADDOCK & SPINACH CHOWDER TART

SERVES 4
PREPARATION & COOKING TIME:
40 minutes + 30 minutes chilling
+ 45–50 minutes cooking
FREEZING: recommended

Wholemeal pastry gives this flan a **delicious flavour and nutty texture**. Adding baking powder ensures a much lighter result than you would expect. This is a good recipe for the summer months when courgettes are at their best. Slices of this flan make great picnic fare. Alternatively, you could serve this warm with a tomato salsa.

COURGETTE & GRUYÈRE FLAN

FOR THE WHOLEMEAL PASTRY:
115 g (4 oz) wholemeal flour
1 teaspoon baking powder
25 g (1 oz) butter or block margarine
25 g (1 oz) lard or white vegetable fat

FOR THE FILLING:
15 g (½ oz) butter
1 small onion, halved and sliced thinly
225 g (8 oz) courgettes, sliced into ½ cm (¼-inch) rings
1 teaspoon chopped fresh thyme
80 g (3 oz) Gruyère cheese, grated
2 large eggs
300 ml (10 fl oz) double cream
salt and freshly ground black pepper

1 For the pastry, mix the flour and baking powder together in a bowl. Rub in the butter and lard or vegetable fat. Stir in 2 tablespoons cold water and bring it all together to form a ball of dough.

2 On a lightly floured surface roll out the pastry and use it to line a deep 20 cm (8-inch) flan tin. Prick the base with a fork and chill for at least 30 minutes.

3 Preheat the oven to Gas Mark 6/ electric oven 200°C/fan oven 180°C. Place a baking sheet on the middle shelf.

4 For the filling, melt the butter in a frying-pan and add the onion and courgettes. Sauté for about 5 minutes, until the onion has softened and the courgettes have started to turn golden.

5 Bake the pastry case blind for 15 minutes. Remove the foil or paper and beans and return to the oven for a further 5 minutes.

6 Scatter the courgette mixture over the pastry base and sprinkle with the thyme and grated cheese. Whisk together the eggs, cream and seasoning, and pour this into the flan case. Bake in the oven for 30–35 minutes, until puffy and golden.

SERVES 4
PREPARATION & COOKING TIME:
25 minutes + 30 minutes chilling
+ 25–30 minutes cooking
FREEZING: recommended

Ask anyone to name a quiche and this rich bacon and egg tart will immediately spring to mind. As with many classic recipes **it is open to variations** – for instance grated cheese is often included. Here I have used a cheese pastry instead of the traditional shortcrust. The cheese subtly flavours the tart and gives it a lovely golden colour.

QUICHE LORRAINE

FOR THE CHEESE PASTRY:
115 g (4 oz) plain flour
½ teaspoon dry mustard
25 g (1 oz) butter
25 g (1 oz) lard
50 g (2 oz) Cheddar cheese, grated finely

FOR THE FILLING:
115 g (4 oz) smoked streaky bacon
2 large eggs + 1 large yolk, beaten
300 ml (10 fl oz) double cream
salt and freshly ground black pepper

1   For the pastry; sift together the flour and mustard. Rub in the butter and lard. Stir in the cheese, and mix to a soft, stiff dough with 2 tablespoons cold water.

2   Roll out the dough on a lightly floured surface and use it to line a deep 20 cm (8-inch) flan tin. Prick the base with a fork and chill for 30 minutes.

3   Preheat the oven to Gas Mark 6/electric oven 200°C/fan oven 180°C. Place a baking sheet on the centre shelf.

4   On the warmed baking sheet, bake the pastry case blind for 15 minutes. Remove the foil or paper and baking beans, and cook for a further 5 minutes. Remove from the oven and reduce the oven temperature to Gas Mark 5/electric oven 190°C/fan oven 170°C.

5   Meanwhile make the filling. Cook the bacon in a frying-pan for 3–4 minutes until cooked, but not crisp. Using scissors, cut it into bite-sized pieces.

6   Whisk the beaten eggs and yolk with the cream, and season with salt and pepper (depending how salty the bacon is).

7   Scatter the bacon over the base of the pastry case. Return it to the oven and, with the shelf half way out of the oven, carefully pour in the cream mixture. Slowly slide the shelf back into the oven, and bake for 25–30 minutes, until the filling is just set.

SERVES 4
PREPARATION & COOKING TIME:
20 minutes + 30 minutes chilling
+ 30 minutes cooking
FREEZING: not recommended

Imagine those favourite cooked breakfast ingredients, all encapsulated in a quiche. What's more it has a case made of sliced bread which, when cooked, is crispy just like fried bread. This would make an ideal brunch or a Sunday night supper dish.

FOR THE BREAD CASE:
6 medium slices of bread from a
square cut white loaf
40 g (1½ oz) butter, softened

FOR THE FILLING:
1 teaspoon sunflower oil
175 g (6 oz) good quality pork chipolatas,
cut into bite-sized pieces
80 g (3 oz) lean streaky bacon, snipped
80 g (3 oz) button mushrooms, wiped
50 g (2 oz) cherry tomatoes, halved
2 large eggs, beaten
300 ml (10 fl oz) milk
salt and freshly ground black pepper

1   Remove and discard the crusts from the bread. Spread the slices thinly with some of the butter and arrange them, butter side down, in a 20 cm (8-inch) square or 23 cm (9-inch) round cake tin. Make sure that the bread is pressed together well so that there are no gaps for the liquid to disappear down. Spread the remaining butter over the inside of the bread case to form a seal. Chill for 30 minutes.

2   Preheat the oven to Gas Mark 5/electric oven 190°C/fan oven 170°C.

3   Heat the oil in a frying pan and add the sausage pieces. Fry them over a medium-high heat for 3–4 minutes, until browned. Add the bacon and fry for a couple of minutes until crisp. Now add the mushrooms to the pan (halve any large ones) and cook for 1 minute.

4   Remove any excess fat with kitchen paper and scatter the fried ingredients over the base of the quiche. Arrange the tomato halves on top.

5   Whisk together the eggs and milk and season with salt and pepper. Pour into the bread case.

6   Bake in the middle of the oven for about 30 minutes, or until the quiche is puffy and golden. Serve at once.

THE GREAT ENGLISH BREAKFAST QUICHE

SERVES 4–6
PREPARATION & COOKING TIME:
15 minutes + 30 minutes chilling
+ 50 minutes cooking
FREEZING: not recommended

Although not strictly an authentic Scottish tart, this recipe does make use of two of its greatest products – smoked salmon and oatmeal. **A tangy watercress and orange salad would complement this flan's rich flavour perfectly**.

FOR THE OATMEAL PASTRY:
50 g (2 oz) medium oatmeal
50 g (2 oz) plain flour
a good pinch of salt
25 g (1 oz) butter
25 g (1 oz) lard

FOR THE FILLING:
175 g (6 oz) smoked salmon pieces
2 large eggs, beaten
500 g carton of plain fromage frais
2 tablespoons snipped chives
salt and freshly ground black pepper

1 To make the pastry, mix together the oatmeal, flour and salt. Rub in the butter and lard, and then add 2 tablespoons cold water and mix to a soft dough.
2 Roll out the pastry and use it to line a 20 cm (8-inch) deep, loose-bottomed flan tin. Prick the base with a fork. Chill for at least 30 minutes.
3 Preheat the oven to Gas Mark 6/electric oven 200°C/fan oven 180°C. Place a baking sheet on the middle shelf.
4 On the warmed baking sheet, bake the pastry case blind for 15 minutes. Remove the foil or paper and beans, and return it to the oven for a further 5 minutes.
5 Scatter smoked salmon over the base of tart. Whisk together beaten eggs, fromage frais and chives. Season the mixture and pour this over the salmon. Return the flan to the oven for a further 30 minutes, until the filling is just set.

SCOTTISH SALMON FLAN

SERVES 4
PREPARATION & COOKING TIME:
25 minutes + 30 minutes chilling
+ 45–60 minutes cooking
FREEZING: recommended

This is a real Cinderella dish! The pastry base uses potato, which makes a lovely soft dough to handle and, when cooked, browns to a chip-like golden colour. If you do not have a microwave, boil the potatoes for the filling in advance, adding an extra one for the pastry.

FOR THE POTATO PASTRY:
1 medium (115 g/4 oz) floury potato
115 g (4 oz) plain flour
1 teaspoon baking powder
a pinch of salt
40 g (1½ oz) butter
40 g (1½ oz) lard
1 large egg yolk

FOR THE FILLING:
350 g (12 oz) potatoes, peeled
1 tablespoon olive oil
25 g (1 oz) butter
450 g (1 lb) onions, chopped
1 garlic clove, peeled
¼ teaspoon salt
45 ml (3 tablespoons) double cream
1 teaspoon Dijon mustard
115 g (4 oz) Cheddar cheese, grated
3 tablespoons chopped fresh parsley
freshly ground black pepper

1 To make the pastry, wash the potato and wrap it in a piece of kitchen paper. Microwave on HIGH for 4 minutes, turning it half way through cooking. Allow it to cool before removing its skin and mashing with a fork, until smooth as possible.

2 Combine the flour, baking powder and salt in a bowl. Rub in the butter and lard. Stir in the mashed potato. Add the egg yolk and bring it all together to form a ball of dough.

3 Roll out the dough on a lightly floured surface and use it to line a deep 20 cm (8-inch) loose-bottomed flan ring. Prick the base all over with a fork and chill for at least 30 minutes.

4 Preheat the oven to Gas Mark 7/electric oven 220°C/fan oven 200°C. Place a baking sheet on the middle shelf.

5 To make the filling, boil the potatoes for about 15 minutes, until just tender. Drain and slice them thinly.

6 Meanwhile, heat the oil and butter in a pan and sauté the onion for 10–15 minutes, until it is transparent and softened – do not allow it to brown.

7 Using a pestle and mortar, pound the garlic and salt to a creamy consistency. Add the cream, mustard and pepper to the garlic purée.

8 Layer the potato, onion, grated cheese and parsley in the pastry case, reserving 25 g (1 oz) cheese for the top. Pour in the garlicky cream mixture.

9 Sprinkle the top with the remaining grated cheese. Place the tin on the heated baking sheet and cook for 25–30 minutes, until the pastry is crisp and the top is golden.

FARMHOUSE POTATO PIE

SERVES 4
PREPARATION & COOKING TIME:
15 minutes + 40–45 minutes cooking
FREEZING: not recommended

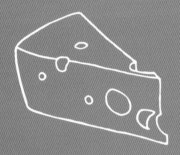

This tart is based on the classic Greek pie recipe.

For this version I have included a mixture of ricotta, feta and Parmesan, and the filo pastry sheets are brushed with melted butter, rather than olive oil. A salad of roughly chopped tomatoes with vinaigrette dressing, and crusty, warm bread would be ideal accompaniments.

SPINACH & THREE CHEESE FILO TART

25 g (1 oz) butter
350 g (12 oz) spinach, ready washed
1 teaspoon olive oil
a bunch of spring onions, sliced
115 g (4 oz) feta cheese, crumbled
115 g (4 oz) ricotta cheese
50 g (2 oz) Parmesan cheese, grated
1 tablespoon finely chopped fresh parsley
¼ freshly grated nutmeg
1 large egg plus 1 large yolk, beaten
3 x 40 cm x 23 cm (16 inches x 9 inches) sheets filo pastry
freshly ground black pepper

1 Preheat the oven to Gas Mark 5/electric oven 190°C/fan oven 170°C. Place a baking sheet in the centre of the oven.

2 Melt a small knob of the butter in a large saucepan. Add the spinach and cook it quickly for 1–2 minutes, until wilted. Drain and cool slightly. Squeeze out any remaining liquid, chop and put it in a mixing bowl.

3 Heat the olive oil in a small saucepan and soften the spring onions without browning them. Add them to the spinach along with the feta, ricotta, Parmesan (reserving 2 tablespoons), parsley, nutmeg and pepper. Taste the mixture to check the seasoning and then stir in the egg and yolk.

4 Melt the remaining butter and use a little to grease a 20 cm (8-inch) round cake tin. Brush all three filo sheets with melted butter and arrange them in the tin, one at a time, laying them at angles, so that there are no gaps. Gently press the sheets into the bottom rim of the tin.

5 Spoon the filling into the prepared pastry case and sprinkle the top with the reserved Parmesan. Roll up the overhanging pastry to form an edge and brush with butter. Bake for 40–45 minutes, until the pastry is golden and the filling is set. Allow it to settle in the tin for 10 minutes before cutting.

Although the basic idea of what makes a tart has remained unchanged, the style of presentation and range of ingredients now available has opened up new and exciting possibilities.

In this chapter, I have endeavoured to update your repertoire with simple, quick tarts, incorporating ingredients that, only a few years ago, were hard to find. Here we take advantage of the wonderful variety of cheeses found on the dairy shelves of

TODAY'S TARTS

supermarkets. Garlic Mushroom and Taleggio Tart features the creamy Italian cheese Taleggio, and Pont L'Evêque is a key flavour in Asparagus, Melted Cheese and Parma Ham Galette. Cheese and pastry really bring out the best in each other. Once you try out some of these ideas for yourself you'll see what I mean!

SERVES 6–8
PREPARATION & COOKING TIME:
20 minutes + 45 minutes proving
+ about 1 hour cooking
FREEZING: recommended

How did we ever survive without roasted vegetables?

So much concentrated flavour for so little effort! The base of this tart is dough which soaks up those delicious juices from the tomatoes and peppers so well. Vary the choice of vegetables to suit your taste.

FOR THE DOUGH BASE:
**175 g (6 oz) plain flour
1 teaspoon easy blend yeast
¼ teaspoon salt
1 large egg, beaten
2 tablespoons olive oil**

FOR THE TOPPING:
**450 g (1 lb) tomatoes, quartered
1 red and 1 yellow pepper, de-seeded
and cut into chunks
1 small red onion, peeled and
sliced into wedges
½ head of garlic
2–3 sprigs rosemary
2 tablespoons olive oil
1 tablespoon pine kernels
10 black olives
salt and freshly ground black pepper**

1 Preheat the oven to Gas Mark 9/electric oven 250°C/fan oven 230°C.

2 Combine the flour, yeast and salt in a bowl. Make a well in the centre and add the egg, 50 ml (2 fl oz) warm water and oil. Stir it all to form a dough. Turn out the dough and knead it for 5 minutes until smooth. Place it in an oiled polythene bag, and leave in a warm place to prove for about 45 minutes.

3 To make the filling, place the tomatoes, peppers and onion in a roasting tray. Break the garlic into cloves, don't peel them just remove the papery layer. Add them to the tray along with the rosemary. Season and add the olive oil, tossing well to coat all the vegetables. Roast for about 40 minutes on the top shelf of the oven turning the vegetables once, until their edges are charred. Remove from the oven and allow the vegetables to cool. Reduce the oven temperature to Gas Mark 6/electric oven 200°C/fan oven 180°C.

4 Grease a 26 cm (10½-inch) round, loose-bottomed tin or pizza tray, and then using your fingertips, press the dough into its base.

5 Slice the base off the garlic cloves, squeeze the tips and a creamy purée should pop out easily. Spread this over the top of the dough. Spoon over the roasted vegetables along with their juices. Sprinkle with pine kernels and dot with olives. Bake in the centre of the oven for 15–20 minutes, until risen and golden.

MEDITERRANEAN ROASTED VEGETABLE TART

SERVES 4
PREPARATION & COOKING TIME:
20 minutes + 45 minutes proving + 45–55 minutes cooking
FREEZING: recommended

RED ONION & GOAT'S CHEESE PIZZA TART

The combination of red onion, balsamic vinegar and goat's cheese is now an established one, so I have included my own variation to serve as a light lunch or supper dish. This tart also slices very well, so you could offer bite-sized pieces as appetisers.

FOR THE DOUGH BASE:
175 g (6 oz) plain flour
1 teaspoon easy blend yeast
¼ teaspoon salt
1 large egg, beaten
2 tablespoons extra virgin olive oil

FOR THE TOPPING:
1 tablespoon olive oil
2 medium red onions, halved and sliced thinly
2 teaspoons chopped fresh thyme, plus extra to garnish
2 tablespoons balsamic vinegar
2 teaspoons granulated sugar
120 g roll of goat's cheese
salt and freshly ground black pepper

1 Preheat the oven to Gas Mark 6/electric oven 200°C/fan oven 180°C.
2 Combine the flour, yeast and salt. Make a well in the centre, add the egg, 50 ml (2 fl oz) warm water and oil, and mix to form a dough. Turn out the dough and knead for 5 minutes until smooth. Place in an oiled polythene bag, seal and leave in a warm place to prove for about 45 minutes.
3 For the topping, heat the oil and sweat the onions and thyme over a medium heat, uncovered, for 25–30 minutes, until softened.
4 Add the vinegar and sugar, increase the heat, and boil for about 5 minutes, until the mixture is syrupy and the onions start to caramelise. Season to taste.
5 Using your fingertips, press the risen dough into the base of a greased shallow baking tray, measuring 25 cm x 17 cm (10 inches x 6½ inches). Spread the onion mixture over the surface.
6 If using hard goat's cheese, discard the ends, and slice it thinly into 12 rounds. Dot the slices over the onion mixture.
7 Bake in the centre of the oven for about 20 minutes until risen and golden. Scatter a few stalks of thyme over the top and serve at once.

SERVES 6
PREPARATION & COOKING TIME:
25 minutes + 30 minutes chilling + about 1 hour cooking
FREEZING: recommended

SERVES 6
PREPARATION & COOKING TIME:
15 minutes + 25–30 minutes cooking
FREEZING: recommended

LEEK, CHORIZO & GRUYÈRE TART

GARLIC MUSHROOM & TALEGGIO TART

Chorizo is a spicy Spanish sausage seasoned with paprika and garlic, its intense flavour gives a real kick to this tart. If you prefer a less distinctive taste, pancetta makes a good substitute – you can cook it in the same way. Serve this tart warm.

This is one of my favourite tarts because it's so easy and quick to prepare – and so delicious. You could even make mini ones to serve with drinks – ideal for Christmas time when you have 101 other things to do!

FOR THE PASTRY:
shortcrust pastry made using 115 g (4 oz) plain flour (page 10)

FOR THE PASTRY:
375 g packet of ready rolled puff pastry

FOR THE FILLING:
175 g (6 oz) baby leeks, washed
1 teaspoon olive oil
115 g (4 oz) chorizo sausage, diced into 1 cm (½ inch) cubes
115 g (4 oz) Gruyère cheese, grated
300 ml (10 fl oz) milk
2 large eggs + 1 large yolk, beaten
salt and freshly ground black pepper

FOR THE FILLING:
70 g (2½ oz) butter
450 g (1 lb) mushrooms, sliced (dark gilled ones are best)
2 garlic cloves, sliced thinly
4 tablespoons chopped fresh parsley
1 egg, beaten lightly
200 g packet of Taleggio cheese, cut into 12 slices
salt and freshly ground black pepper

1 Line a shallow 23 cm (9-inch) flan ring with the shortcrust pastry and chill for 30 minutes.
2 Preheat the oven to Gas Mark 5/electric oven 190°C/fan oven 170°C. Place a baking tray on the centre shelf.
3 Trim all but 2.5 cm (1 inch) of green from the end of the leeks. Heat the oil in a frying-pan. Fry the leeks with the chorizo for 3–4 minutes, turning, until the sausage is crisp and golden. Drain on kitchen paper.
4 On the heated baking sheet, bake the pastry case blind for 15 minutes. Remove the foil or paper and beans and cook for a further 5 minutes.
5 Scatter chorizo over the pastry base. Sprinkle the cheese over the top, and arrange the leeks in a pinwheel shape, whites inwards. Whisk together the milk, eggs and seasoning. Pour this into the pastry case and bake for 30–35 minutes, until puffy and set.

1 Preheat the oven to Gas Mark 6/electric oven 200°C/fan oven 180°C.
2 Melt the butter in a large frying pan and add the sliced mushrooms with the garlic. Fry gently for about 5 minutes, or until all the liquid has evaporated.
3 Season and add 3 tablespoons of the chopped parsley to the pan.
4 Divide the pastry into six rectangles, measuring approximately 14 cm x 11 cm (5½ inches x 4¼ inches). Score a line, about 1 cm (½ inch) in from the edge of each rectangle. Place the pastries on a baking sheet, pricking each one all over with a fork. Brush them with beaten egg.
5 Divide the mushroom topping between the pastry bases within the scored border. Place a couple of slices of Taleggio on top of each and bake for 20–25 minutes, until the cheese has melted and the pastries are golden. Serve with a scattering of chopped parsley over each.

SERVES 4
PREPARATION AND COOKING TIME:
40 minutes + 15 minutes cooling sauce
+ 30 minutes cooking
FREEZING: Not recommended

This tart is simply **bursting with both colour and flavour** and is easy to make. Olive oil is used in place of butter and lard in the pastry, making a crisp shell, which holds its shape well. This tart is a main course by itself.

FOR THE PASTRY:
175 g (6 oz) plain flour
a pinch of salt
4 tablespoons extra virgin olive oil

FOR THE TOPPING:
1 tablespoon olive oil
350 g (12 oz) plum tomatoes, skinned and chopped roughly
1 garlic clove, peeled
¼ teaspoon sea salt
1 teaspoon sherry vinegar
½ teaspoon chopped fresh oregano or ¼ teaspoon dried oregano
½ teaspoon brown sugar
bay leaf
200 g can of tuna chunks or steaks, drained
2 teaspoons capers
25 g (1 oz) rocket leaves
25 g (1 oz) Parmesan cheese shavings
freshly ground black pepper

1   To make the pastry, combine the flour and salt in a mixing bowl. Add the oil, and enough cold water (about 4 tablespoons) to bind. Bring the mixture together with your hands, and work very gently, using your fingertips, to make a soft dough.

2   Break off small pieces of dough at a time and press them into the bottom, and 2 cm (¾ inch) up the sides, of a 23 cm (9-inch) shallow, loose-bottomed, flan tin. Prick well with a fork and chill while you make the tomato sauce.

3   Heat the oil and add the tomatoes. Using a pestle and mortar pound the garlic and salt to a creamy consistency. Add this to the tomato mixture with the vinegar, oregano, sugar and bay leaf. Season with pepper. Simmer, uncovered, for about 30 minutes, until the mixture is pulpy. You may need to turn up the heat for the last 5 minutes to evaporate the liquid.

4   Preheat the oven to Gas Mark 6/electric oven 200°C/fan oven 180°C. Place a baking sheet on the middle shelf.

5   Cool the tomato sauce for about 15 minutes before spreading it over the pastry base. Scatter the tuna chunks over the top. Bake for about 30 minutes until the pastry is crisp and golden.

6   Remove the tart from the oven, sprinkle with capers and scatter rocket and Parmesan shavings over the surface.

TUNA TART WITH WILTED ROCKET & PARMESAN SHAVINGS

SERVES 6
PREPARATION & COOKING TIME:
10 minutes + 20–25 minutes cooking
FREEZING: recommended

This is a special tart for entertaining. Asparagus is always a luxury and combined with Parma ham, and creamy Pont L'Evêque cheese you have a quick, yet sumptuous dish. Petit Pont L'Evêque can be bought in a small, 220 g, box in which case you will need to use three quarters. Camembert or Brie could be substituted if they are more readily available.

FOR THE PASTRY:
225 g (8 oz) ready rolled puff pastry
1 egg, beaten

FOR THE FILLING:
115 g (4 oz) asparagus tips
5 ml (1 teaspoon) olive oil
1 teaspoon lemon juice
6 slices (approximately 80 g/3 oz) Parma or Serrano ham
175 g (6 oz) Petit Pont L'Evêque
salt and freshly ground black pepper

1   Preheat the oven to Gas Mark 6/electric oven 200°C/fan oven 180°C.
2   Trim the ends of the asparagus. Blanch the stems in boiling water for 2 minutes, drain and toss them in the olive oil and lemon juice. Season and leave to cool.
3   Cut each slice of ham longways. Wrap each asparagus stalk in a piece of ham – don't worry if you have a few stems spare, they can just be popped on the tart anyway.
4   Unroll the pastry from its packaging and lay it on a baking sheet. Using a sharp knife, score a line 1 cm (½ inch) from the edge. Prick the middle well with a fork, and brush it all over with the beaten egg.
5   Arrange the asparagus rolls on the pastry within the scored border; lay any spare asparagus tips in between. Remove and discard the edges of the cheese and thinly slice it. Arrange the cheese slices over the asparagus. Season with freshly ground black pepper.
6   Bake in the centre of the oven for 20–25 minutes, until the pastry is puffy and golden, and the cheese is bubbly and melted. Serve at once.

ASPARAGUS, MELTED CHEESE & PARMA HAM GALETTE

There are many favourites here, which I hope you will enjoy. Perhaps the chapter would have been better titled 'Pastries that Grandma Used to Bake'! Bakewell Tart and Strawberry Shortcake certainly live up to that description, while Pecan Pie has long been made by American Grandmas. You'll also find here a large version of the very English, Baked Custard Tart usually found as individual little tarts. I have suggested accompanying this with caramel oranges.

TRADITIONAL TARTS

Some of these tarts use either a rich sweet flan pastry, or pâte sucrée. If you are put off by having to make these pastries yourself, then please substitute bought shortcrust instead or buy a ready-made sweet shortcrust flan case.

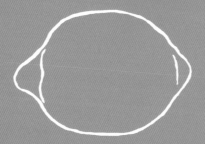

SERVES 6
PREPARATION & COOKING TIME:
40 minutes + 30 minutes chilling
+ 35–40 minutes baking
FREEZING: not recommended

This is an all time **English classic**, passed down from generation to generation. The tartness of the lemon filling is offset by a flurry of sweet meringue.

LEMON MERINGUE PIE

FOR THE PASTRY:
**shortcrust pastry made with 115 g
(4 oz) plain flour (page 10)**

FOR THE FILLING:
**25 g (1 oz) cornflour
grated zest and juice of 2 lemons,
300 ml (10 fl oz) water
115 g (4 oz) caster sugar
50 g (2 oz) unsalted butter
2 large egg yolks**

FOR THE MERINGUE:
**2 large egg whites
80 g (3 oz) caster sugar**

1   Line a 20 cm (8-inch) loose-bottomed, deep flan tin with the shortcrust pastry and chill for 30 minutes.
2   Preheat the oven to Gas Mark 6/electric oven 200°C/fan oven 180°C. Place a baking sheet on the middle shelf.
3   On the heated baking sheet, bake the pastry case blind for 15 minutes. Remove the foil or paper and beans and return to the oven for a further 5–10 minutes, until cooked. Turn down the oven temperature to Gas Mark 2/electric oven 150°C/fan oven 130°C.
4   Mix the cornflour to a smooth paste with lemon juice.
5   Pour the water into a saucepan and add the lemon zest and sugar. Stir over a gentle heat until dissolved. Turn up the heat and bring to the boil. Pour this on to the cornflour mixture, whisking constantly.

Return it all to the saucepan and beat for 1 minute, until you have a thick, smooth consistency. Cool slightly, and then beat in the butter and egg yolks.
6   Pour the lemon filling into the pastry case and allow to cool for about 5 minutes to firm it up slightly.
7   To make the meringue, whisk the egg whites until they are stiff. Gradually beat in half the sugar, and then carefully fold in the remainder, reserving 1 teaspoon. Spread the meringue mixture over the filling, making sure to cover the pastry edges as well. Swirl with a palette knife to make peaks. Sprinkle with the reserved sugar and bake for 35–40 minutes, until the meringue is crisp. Serve warm.

SERVES 6
PREPARATION & COOKING TIME:
20 minutes + 30 minutes chilling + about 1 hour cooking
FREEZING: not recommended

PECAN PIE

I always think that if you are going to have a pudding, you might as well enjoy it and not count the cost. It looks good, tastes great, and is as easy as pie to make. Serve it with whipped cream – and enjoy!

FOR THE PASTRY:
shortcrust pastry made with 115 g (4 oz) plain flour (page 10)

FOR THE FILLING:
2 large eggs, beaten
115 g (4 oz) light muscovado sugar
115 g (4 oz) golden syrup
1 teaspoon vanilla extract
25 g (1 oz) unsalted butter, melted
25 g (1 oz) plain flour
175 g (6 oz) pecan nuts
1 tablespoon apricot jam, warmed and sieved

1 Line a deep 20 cm (8-inch) flan tin with the shortcrust pastry. Chill for 30 minutes.
2 Preheat the oven to Gas Mark 6/electric oven 200°C/fan oven 180°C. Put a baking sheet on the middle shelf of the oven.
3 On the heated baking sheet, bake the pastry case blind for 15 minutes, remove the foil or paper and beans and cook for a further 5–10 minutes, until the pastry is cooked.
4 To make the filling, combine the eggs, sugar, syrup and vanilla in a bowl. Stir in the butter and flour.
5 Chop 115 g (4 oz) of the pecan nuts and add these to the bowl.
6 Reduce the oven temperature to Gas Mark 4/electric oven 180°C/fan oven 160°C. Pour the filling into the pastry case and arrange the remaining whole pecan nuts on the top. Bake for 30–35 minutes until the filling is set and browned.
7 Brush with apricot jam and serve warm.

SERVES 8
PREPARATION & COOKING TIME:
10 minutes + 30 minutes cooking
FREEZING: recommended

BAKEWELL TART

It is no wonder that this tart has stood the test of time. It doubles up as a pudding or teatime treat, and is simplicity itself to make. I have used puff pastry here, but shortcrust can also be used.

FOR THE PASTRY:
225 g (8 oz) ready-made puff pastry

FOR THE FILLING:
3 slightly rounded tablespoons raspberry jam
2 large eggs plus 2 large yolks
115 g (4 oz) unsalted butter, melted
115 g (4 oz) caster sugar
115 g (4 oz) ground almonds
a few drops of almond essence
flaked almonds, to decorate

1 Preheat the oven to Gas Mark 6/electric oven 200°C/fan oven 180°C. Place a baking sheet on the middle shelf.
2 On a lightly floured surface roll out the pastry and use it to line a 20 cm (8-inch) loose-bottomed, deep flan tin. Prick well with a fork.
3 Spread jam over the base of the pastry case.
4 Place the eggs and yolks in a bowl. Beat gently to just combine them. Trickle in the slightly cooled melted butter, stirring constantly. Add the sugar and almonds and just a few drops of almond essence for flavour.
5 Pour the mixture into the pastry case and scatter flaked almonds over the surface. Bake (on the heated baking sheet) for about 30 minutes, or until the centre is just firm to the touch. Allow to cool for at least half an hour before serving warm.

SERVES 8–10
PREPARATION & COOKING TIME:
25 minutes +1 hour chilling
+ 40–45 minutes cooking
FREEZING: not recommended

This is one of those tarts that you'd see in the window of a pâtisserie or coffee house **to tempt you** inside. Pear fans, artistically arranged over a walnut batter, glisten with an apricot glaze. Ground almonds can be substituted for the walnuts and apples, and apricots or plums work equally as well as pears. Serve it warm with a generous dollop of crème fraîche.

FOR THE PASTRY:
**pâte sucrée made using 175 g (6 oz) flour
(page 11)**

FOR THE FILLING:
**80 g (3 oz) unsalted butter
80 g (3 oz) caster sugar
½ teaspoon vanilla essence
2 large eggs, lightly beaten
80 g (3 oz) walnuts, ground
in a liquidizer
3–4 ripe pears, Comice are ideal**

FOR THE GLAZE:
**2 tablespoons apricot jam, sieved
1 tablespoon lemon juice**

1   Line a 23 cm (9-inch) loose-bottomed, deep flan tin with the pâte sucrée. Chill for 1 hour.
2   Preheat the oven to Gas Mark 5/electric oven 190°C/fan oven 170°C. Put a baking sheet on the middle shelf for the tart.
3   To make the filling, cream the butter and sugar with the vanilla essence until the mixture is pale. Fold in the beaten eggs along with the ground walnuts, a little at a time (this helps prevent the mixture from curdling).
4   Spread the walnut paste over the base of the pastry case. Peel, halve and core the pears. Cut them thinly into 8–10 slices, leaving 1 cm (½ inch) uncut at the top so that the sections are held together. Gently ease out the pear halves into fans, and arrange them on top of the filling.
5   Bake the tart on the heated baking sheet for 15 minutes. Reduce the oven temperature to Gas Mark 4/electric oven 180°C/fan oven 160°C and cook for a further 25–30 minutes.
6   Blend together the apricot jam and lemon juice. Remove the tart from the oven and, while still hot, brush over the glaze – this prevents the pears from discolouring.

PEAR & WALNUT TART

MAKES 12
PREPARATION & COOKING TIME:
20 minutes + 30 minutes chilling
+ 15 minutes cooking
FREEZING: recommended

There must have been countless variations of mince pies concocted over the years – and here is another! Open-topped tarts look attractive, especially when they feature **rich, glistening mincemeat** decorated with a star or holly leaf. If you are not a fan of marzipan, there will be enough pastry trimmings left over to stamp out shapes. Serve these warm with brandy butter or lightly whipped double cream, flavoured with Cointreau.

FOR THE PASTRY:
115 g (4 oz) plain flour
grated zest of ½ orange + ½ lemon
50 g (2 oz) unsalted butter
25 g (1 oz) caster sugar
1 large egg yolk

FOR THE FILLING:
350 g (12 oz) luxury mincemeat
80 g (3 oz) white marzipan

1   Combine the flour and citrus zests in a bowl. Rub in the butter and then stir in the sugar. Bind it all to a dough with the egg yolk and 1 tablespoon cold water.
2   Roll out the dough on a lightly floured surface. Stamp out 12 rounds using an 8 cm (3¼-inch) round pastry cutter, re-rolling pastry if necessary. Place the rounds in a patty tin. Chill for at least 30 minutes.
3   Preheat the oven to Gas Mark 5/electric oven 190°C/fan oven 170°C.
4   Spoon a heaped teaspoon of mincemeat into each pastry case. Roll out the marzipan on a sugared surface and cut out star or holly shapes. Place a shape in the centre of each tart.
5   Bake the mince pies in the middle of the oven for about 15 minutes, or until the pastry is golden.

MINCE PIES WITH CITRUS PASTRY

SERVES 6
PREPARATION & COOKING TIME:
40 minutes + 30 minutes chilling
+ 35 minutes cooking
FREEZING: not recommended

This is a very old recipe – Apple Amber – traditionally made with just apples. My guess is that its name comes from the orange colour which the brown sugar turns the apples. This version includes blackberries, hence I have called it Ruby Amber Pie.

FOR THE PASTRY:
shortcrust pastry made with 115 g (4 oz)
plain flour (page 10)

FOR THE FILLING:
450 g (1 lb) cooking apples
preferably Bramley's
80 g (3 oz) light muscovado sugar
grated zest and juice of ½ lemon
25 g (1 oz) butter
2 large eggs, separated
175 g (6 oz) blackberries
80 g (3 oz) golden caster sugar

1   Line a 20 cm (8-inch) loose-bottomed, deep flan tin with the shortcrust pastry and chill for 30 minutes.
2   Preheat the oven to Gas Mark 6/electric oven 200°C/fan oven 180°C. Place a baking sheet on the middle shelf.
3   On the heated baking sheet, bake the pastry case blind for 15 minutes, remove the foil and beans and cook for a further 5–10 minutes. Remove from the oven and reduce the heat to Gas Mark 2/electric oven 150°C/fan oven 130°C.
4   Peel, core and slice the apples. Put them in a pan with the muscovado sugar, lemon zest, lemon juice and 1 tablespoon water. Cover and stew for about 15 minutes, until the apples are soft.
5   Allow the apple mixture to cool slightly before beating it to a purée. Beat in the butter followed by the egg yolks, adding them one at a time. Gently stir in the blackberries.
6   In a clean, dry bowl whisk the egg whites until they are stiff. Whisk in a quarter of the golden caster sugar. Add another quarter and whisk again. Fold in the remainder, reserving 1 teaspoon.
7   Spoon the apple and blackberry mixture into the pastry case. Swirl the meringue mixture on top, spreading it to the edges of the pastry, making sure to seal the filling in. Sprinkle with the remaining sugar and bake in the oven for about 35 minutes, until the meringue is risen and golden. Serve warm.

RUBY AMBER PIE

SERVES 6
PREPARATION & COOKING TIME:
20 minutes + 30 minutes chilling + 30–35 minutes cooking
FREEZING: not recommended

OLD FASHIONED TREACLE TART

This recipe needs no introduction: treacle tart has stood the test of time! Arguably one of the most potent reminders of school dinners, it remains as popular as ever today.

FOR THE PASTRY:
shortcrust pastry made with 175 g (6 oz) flour (page 10)

FOR THE FILLING:
25 g (1 oz) fresh white breadcrumbs
grated zest of 1 lemon
275 g (9$\frac{1}{2}$ oz) golden syrup
milk for brushing

1   Line a 20 cm (8-inch) metal pie plate with the shortcrust pastry, reserving the trimmings for later. Chill for 30 minutes.
2   Preheat the oven to Gas Mark 5/electric oven 190°C/fan oven 170°C. Place a baking sheet in the centre of the oven.
3   Scatter the breadcrumbs and lemon zest over the pastry base.
4   Gently warm the syrup, to make it flow more readily, and pour it over the breadcrumbs.
5   Reroll the pastry trimmings and cut them into 1 cm ($\frac{1}{2}$-inch) wide strips. Twist and lay them across the top of the tart in a lattice pattern. Seal the edges with milk and trim.
6   Brush the pastry with milk and bake for 30–35 minutes on the warmed baking sheet. Allow it to rest for about half an hour to give the syrup a chance to set. Serve warm.

SERVES 8
PREPARATION & COOKING TIME:
20 minutes + 30 minutes chilling + 50 minutes cooking
FREEZING: recommended

CHERRY & ALMOND TART

Amaretto liqueur is the secret of success here, as it is more subtle than the rather harsh-flavoured almond essence often used in this tart. Delicious offered at teatime or as a dessert, it can be served hot or cold. I would serve this in a very English way with some freshly made custard.

FOR THE PASTRY:
sweet rich shortcrust pastry made with 115 g (4 oz) flour (page 10)

FOR THE FILLING:
115 g (4 oz) unsalted butter, softened
115 g (4 oz) caster sugar
115 g (4 oz) ground almonds
25 g (1 oz) self-raising flour
2 large eggs, beaten
1 tablespoon Amaretto
225 g (8 oz) stoned sweet red or black cherries
15 g ($\frac{1}{2}$ oz) flaked almonds

1   Line a 20 cm (8-inch) loose-bottomed, deep flan tin with the sweet rich shortcrust pastry. Chill for 30 minutes.
2   Preheat the oven to Gas Mark 5/electric oven 190°C/fan oven 170°C. Place a baking sheet just above the middle shelf.
3   On the heated baking sheet, bake the pastry case blind for 15 minutes, then remove the foil or paper and beans and return it to the oven for a further 5 minutes.
4   Meanwhile, cream together the butter and sugar. Combine the ground almonds and flour. Beat this into the creamed mixture alternately with the eggs. Add the Amaretto.
5   Scatter the cherries over the pastry base. Spoon over the almond filling and smooth it out. Sprinkle the top with flaked almonds and bake for approximately 30 minutes, until risen and just firm to the touch.

SERVES 8
PREPARATION & COOKING TIME:
25 minutes + 30 minutes chilling + 15 minutes cooking
FREEZING: not recommended

STRAWBERRY SHORTCAKE

This is a very easy pudding, **ideal for hot, sunny days** when you would rather be outside than baking in the kitchen. Make the base the night before and assemble this when required. Raspberries work equally well and can be substituted for the strawberries when they are plentiful.

FOR THE SHORTBREAD:
115 g (4 oz) unsalted butter
75 g (6 oz) self-raising flour
50 g (2 oz) golden caster sugar
1 large egg yolk

FOR THE FILLING:
150 ml (5 fl oz) double cream
200 g carton of plain Greek yogurt
1 tablespoon icing sugar, sifted, plus extra for dusting
a few drops of vanilla essence
450 g (1 lb) strawberries

1 To make the shortbread, rub the butter into the flour, until it resembles fine breadcrumbs. Stir in the sugar and add the egg yolk. Using your hands, mix everything together until the mixture forms a ball.

2 Press pieces of the dough evenly over the base of a greased 23 cm (9-inch) loose-bottomed flan tin, and prick it all over with a fork. Chill for 30 minutes.

3 Preheat the oven to Gas Mark 4/electric oven 180°C/fan oven 160°C. Place a baking tray on the centre shelf of the oven.

4 Bake the shortbread on the heated baking tray for about 15 minutes, or until just lightly coloured. Cool in the tin, and then carefully turn it out on to a serving plate, gently prising it off its base.

5 Pour the cream, yogurt, icing sugar and vanilla essence into a bowl and whisk them together until the mixture leaves a trail. Spread this over the shortcake pastry base.

6 Remove the stalks from the strawberries and arrange them on top of the creamy mixture. Dust with icing sugar to serve.

SERVES 6–8
PREPARATION & COOKING TIME:
25 minutes + 1 hour chilling
+ 70–75 minutes baking
FREEZING: not recommended

This is a large version of the individual custard tarts. The filling should still tremble slightly when you gently shake the pastry case; the **soft, creamy texture** is what really makes this pudding. The caramel oranges offset the delicate flavour of this tart with their bittersweet taste.

FOR THE PASTRY:
pâte sucrée made using 115g (4 oz) plain flour (page 11)

FOR THE FILLING:
300 ml (10 fl oz) single cream
150 ml (5 fl oz) full cream milk
½ cinnamon stick, crushed slightly
¼ teaspoon ground mace
2 large eggs plus 2 large egg yolks, beaten
50 g (2 oz) caster sugar
freshly grated nutmeg

FOR THE CARAMEL ORANGES:
175 g (6 oz) granulated sugar
3 oranges

1　Line a deep 20 cm (8-inch) loose-bottomed, flan tin with the pâte sucrée and chill for 1 hour.
2　Preheat the oven to Gas Mark 5/electric oven 190°C/fan oven 170°C. Place a baking sheet in the centre of the oven.
3　On the warmed baking sheet, bake the pastry case blind for 15 minutes. Remove the foil or paper and beans and continue cooking for a further 5–10 minutes, until the pastry is golden.
4　Meanwhile, pour the cream and milk into a medium saucepan. Put in the piece of cinnamon stick and the mace and bring slowly to the boil.
5　Whisk together the eggs and yolks with the sugar until it is all combined. Strain the hot cream and gradually pour it on to the egg mixture, whisking all the time. Strain this again into a jug.
6　Reduce the oven temperature to Gas Mark 2/electric oven 150°C/fan oven 130°C. Half slide the pastry case into the oven. Carefully pour in the custard and sprinkle it with nutmeg. Slide the shelf back and cook for about 35 minutes, or until the filling is just set.
7　Meanwhile make the caramel oranges. In a heavy-based saucepan, dissolve the sugar over a low heat with 150 ml (5 fl oz) water. Increase the heat and bubble hard for about 15 minutes until you have a golden caramel. You will need to keep an eye on it towards the end as it colours very quickly.
8　Rest the pan in a bowl of cold water, to prevent the caramel cooking further, and with your free hand (wrapped in a tea towel for protection) carefully pour in another 150 ml (5 fl oz) warm water, swilling the pan around to mix it in. Leave to cool.
9　Peel the oranges, removing the pith as well as the skin, and slice them. Place the slices in a glass serving bowl and pour over the cooled caramel.
10　Serve the tart warm with the caramel oranges.

BAKED CUSTARD TART WITH CARAMEL ORANGES

Some of the greatest tarts originate from the Continent and certainly French pâtisserie is second to none. I have not tried to emulate them slavishly, as tarts look and taste quite different when translated into another country's cuisine. The actual flavour of ingredients can differ from country to country – this is particularly true of dairy products as animals' grazing pasture influences the composition of the food. The widespread availability of French-style conserves with their high fruit contents has proved invaluable for creating authentic style tarts, and eliminated the need to make glazes.

CONTINENTAL TARTS

Every recipe in this chapter shines – who would believe that Linzertorte is in essence a jam tart – but so far removed from our English version. Tarte au Citron is unashamedly indulgent using lemons, cream, eggs and sugar. I have also included two (three if you choose to make a traditional Tarte Tatin) apple recipes.

SERVES 6
PREPARATION & COOKING TIME:
25 minutes + 30 minutes chilling
+ 40 minutes cooking
FREEZING: not recommended

Apples are traditionally used for this classic French recipe, but pears are equally delicious. Sometimes I add some ground ginger to the pastry to enhance the warm, comforting feel of this tart. A dollop of crème fraîche is all that's required to finish it off. If you need a shortcut, use bought puff pastry.

FOR THE PASTRY:
50 g (2 oz) unsalted butter
115 g (4 oz) plain flour
1 large egg yolk

FOR THE FILLING:
50 g (2 oz) unsalted butter
115 g (4 oz) caster sugar
4 small firm, ripe pears,
    (approximately 550 g/1¼ lb),
    peeled, quartered and cored

PEAR TARTE TATIN

1 To make the pastry, rub the butter into the flour. Make a well in the mixture and stir in the egg yolk and 1 tablespoon cold water. Bring it all together to form a soft dough. Wrap the dough in clingfilm and chill for at least 30 minutes.

2 Preheat the oven to Gas Mark 6/electric oven 200°C/fan oven 180°C. Place a baking sheet just above the centre of the oven.

3 Melt the butter in a 20 cm (8-inch) saucepan or skillet. Sprinkle over the sugar and arrange the pear quarters on top – cut side uppermost. Cook over a medium high heat for about 20 minutes, or until the pears are fairly dark golden.

4 If you are not using a skillet, arrange the pears, cut side uppermost, in a 20 cm (8-inch) round cake tin. Take a little trouble here as this will be the side of the pudding you will see when it is turned out. Pour over the buttery juices from the pears.

5 On a lightly floured surface roll out the pastry to a 22 cm (8½-inch) round. Lay it on top of the pears in the cake tin, or the skillet, and tuck in the edges.

6 Bake on the heated baking sheet for 20 minutes, or until the pastry is cooked and golden. Leave to stand for 10 minutes before carefully inverting the tart on to a serving dish (the syrup will be very hot). Do not worry if any of the pears are left behind, just remove them carefully and add them into the tart.

NOTE: If using a skillet, place it on a baking tray, as the juices do tend to bubble over the edge a bit.

This is a beautifully textured and flavoured French-style tart that looks stunning. If you are short of time, buy a ready-made sweet pastry case and, in place of the crème pâtissière, combine a 250 g tub of mascarpone with 200 ml (7 fl oz) ready-made fresh custard. This tart is served cold and can be made the day before you plan to serve it.

FOR THE PASTRY:
pâte sucrée made with 115 g (4 oz) plain flour (page 11)

FOR THE FILLING:
3 large eggs
80 g (3 oz) caster sugar
3 tablespoons plain flour
3 tablespoons cornflour
425 ml (¾ pint) milk
a few drops of vanilla extract
411 g can of apricot halves
2 tablespoons apricot jam, sieved

SERVES 6–8
PREPARATION & COOKING TIME:
35 minutes + 1 hour chilling
+ 20–25 minutes cooking
FREEZING: not recommended

CLASSIC APRICOT TART

1   Line a 20 cm (8-inch) loose-bottomed, deep flan tin with the pâte sucrée. Chill for 1 hour.
2   Preheat the oven to Gas Mark 5/electric oven 190°C/fan oven 170°C. Put a baking sheet on the middle shelf.

3   To make the crème pâtissière, whisk together the eggs and sugar in a bowl. Sift together the flour and cornflour, and fold this in to the eggs and sugar. Heat the milk in a medium saucepan to just below boiling. Pour this on to the flour mixture, whisking all the time. Return the sauce to the pan and cook over a low heat, whisking continuously, until it comes to the boil and thickens. (Don't worry if it appears slightly lumpy, keep whisking, and the lumps should disappear.) Stir in the vanilla extract and pour the sauce into a jug. Press a piece of wetted clingfilm on to the surface to prevent a skin from forming, and leave to cool.

4   On the warmed baking sheet, bake the pastry case blind for 15 minutes. Remove the foil or paper and the baking beans and cook for a further 5–10 minutes, until the pastry is lightly browned. Allow to cool.
5   To assemble the tart, carefully remove the pastry case from the tin and place it on a serving plate. Spoon in the crème pâtissière, and smooth it evenly over the pastry base. Drain the canned apricots, pat dry and arrange them over the custard base. Warm the jam and brush it over the apricots to give a lovely glossy finish.

SERVES 10–12
PREPARATION & COOKING TIME:
30 minutes + 1 hour chilling + 1 hour cooking
FREEZING: recommended

My introduction to this tart was as a student staying with relations in the Netherlands. Traditionally it is served warm with mid-morning coffee and the combination of spicy apple and crumbly butter pastry still reminds me of those bright, frosty mornings in early February. So here is Auntie Jenny's recipe as I remember it.

FOR THE PASTRY:
115 g (4 oz) unsalted butter
50 g (2 oz) caster sugar
1 large egg, beaten
175 g (6 oz) self-raising flour

FOR THE FILLING:
80 g (3 oz) sultanas
30 ml (2 tablespoons) Calvados
80 g (3 oz) caster sugar
1 teaspoon mixed spice
900 g (2 lb) cooking apples

DUTCH APPLE CAKE

1 For the pastry, cream together the butter and sugar. Beat in half the egg, and then gradually work in the flour. Turn it all out on to a lightly floured surface and bring together to form a soft dough. Use two thirds of the dough to line a lightly greased 23 cm (9-inch) loose-bottomed, deep flan tin, pressing the pastry over the base and up the sides. (You may find it quicker to roll the pastry, if possible.) Reserve any leftover pastry. Prick the base well with a fork and chill for at least 1 hour. Wrap any reserved pastry in clingfilm.

2 Preheat the oven to Gas Mark 4/electric oven 180°C/fan oven 160°C.

3 Simmer the sultanas in Calvados until the liquid evaporates. If you prefer, you can plump up the fruit by pouring boiling water over instead and leave to soak for 10 minutes, strain.

4 Mix together the sugar and mixed spice. Peel and thinly slice the apples. Scatter one third over the pastry base. Sprinkle over the spicy sugar and one third of the sultanas. Continue layering in this way, ending with sultanas.

5 Roll out the remaining pastry and cut it into strips, approximately 1.5 cm (½ inch) wide. Brush the rim of the tart with some of the remaining beaten egg. Lay the pastry strips at equal intervals over the top of the tart, arranging them to form a lattice pattern. Finally brush beaten egg over all of the pastry.

6 Bake in the centre of the oven for about 1 hour, until the pastry is golden and the apples are soft.

SERVES 8
PREPARATION & COOKING TIME:
20 minutes + at least 1 hour chilling
+ 30 minutes baking
FREEZING: recommended

This Austrian tart takes its name from the town of Linz. Tortes can be defined as somewhere between a biscuit and a tart. This one may be likened to an extremely up-market lattice jam tart, subtly flavoured with cinnamon and lemon zest. Traditionally it is served with whipped cream not just as a dessert, but often with coffee or tea. The dough is very soft and therefore quite tricky to handle, so you could always make it up the night before, refrigerate, and then bake in the morning to serve it warm with coffee – wonderful on a cold winter's day.

115 g (4 oz) unsalted butter, softened
80 g (3 oz) caster sugar
grated zest of ½ lemon
80 g (3 oz) plain flour
½ teaspoon ground cinnamon
80 g (3 oz) ground almonds
or ground hazelnuts
2 large egg yolks
a few drops almond or vanilla essence
225 g (8 oz) red jam or jelly
(raspberry, cranberry or redcurrant)
icing sugar, for dusting

1 Cream the butter, sugar and lemon zest until the mixture is pale and fluffy.
2 Mix together flour, cinnamon and ground nuts. Gradually work them into the creamed mixture, alternating with the egg yolks. Add the almond or vanilla essence. Wrap in clingfilm and chill for at least 1 hour.
3 Preheat the oven to Gas Mark 5/electric oven 190°C/fan oven 170°C. Place a baking sheet on the middle shelf for the tart.
4 Press three-quarters of the dough into the base and 2.5 cm (1 inch) up the sides of a 20 cm (8-inch) loose-bottomed, shallow flan tin. Spread jam or jelly over the base. Add a little more flour to the remaining dough, to make it more manageable, and roll it out fairly thinly. Cut it into strips and lay the strips across the tart to make a lattice effect. Trim the ends and seal the edges, by pressing a fork all the way around the edge.
5 On the warmed baking sheet, bake for about 30 minutes, until golden. Dust with sifted icing sugar and serve warm.

LINZERTORTE

SERVES 10–12
PREPARATION & COOKING TIME:
20 minutes + 1 hour chilling + 50 minutes cooking
FREEZING: not recommended

TARTE AU CITRON

The freshness of this lemon tart gives a real zing to the tastebuds.
I prefer to serve it without a dusting of icing sugar, to show off its pure
yellow colour. Slightly undercook this tart, if anything, and make it the
day before to allow plenty of time for cooling, and chilling overnight.
Delicious served with crème fraîche.

FOR THE PASTRY:
**sweet rich shortcrust pastry made with
115 g (4 oz) plain flour (page 10)**

FOR THE FILLING:
5 large eggs, beaten
150 g (5 oz) caster sugar
grated zest and juice of 5 unwaxed lemons
300 ml (10 fl oz) double cream

1 Line a 23 cm (9-inch) loose-bottomed, deep flan tin with the
   sweet rich shortcrust pastry. Chill for 1 hour.
2 Preheat the oven to Gas Mark 5/electric oven 190°C/fan oven
   170°C. Place a baking sheet in the centre of the oven for the tart.
3 On the warmed baking sheet, bake the pastry case blind for 15
   minutes. Remove the foil or paper and beans and cook for a
   further 5 minutes.
4 Meanwhile, mix the eggs and sugar in a bowl to just combine them.
5 Stir the lemon zest and juice into the bowl followed by the double
   cream.
6 Reduce the oven temperature to Gas Mark 2/electric oven
   150°C/fan oven 130°C. Slide the oven shelf half out for the tart
   and pour the lemon mixture into the pastry case. Very carefully
   slide back the shelf and cook for 30 minutes. The tart should have
   a slight tremor in the centre, but will continue cooking when the
   oven is switched off. Leave the oven door ajar and leave the tart
   inside to cool. Chill thoroughly before serving.

 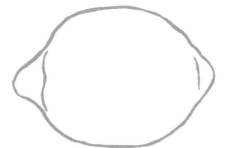 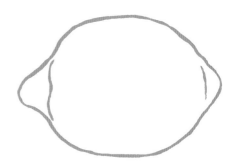

SERVES 8
PREPARATION & COOKING TIME:
25 minutes + 1 hour chilling + 1¼ hours cooking
FREEZING: not recommended

ITALIAN RICOTTA TART

This traditional Italian cheesecake is evocative of Christmas with its candied and dried fruit steeped in Galliano. Pine kernels are strongly flavoured, and can easily be omitted if not to your taste – just use 25 g (1 oz) more fruit. The cocoa pastry, while not authentic, contrasts well with the filling, but you can use the traditional sweet rich shortcrust base if you prefer. A compote of fresh apricots, poached in sugar syrup and flavoured with the zest of lemon, a cinnamon stick and a halved vanilla pod, would make a perfect accompaniment.

FOR THE COCOA PASTRY:

sweet rich shortcrust pastry made with 115 g (4 oz) flour
2 teaspoons cocoa powder sifted with the flour
 and icing sugar (page 10)

FOR THE FILLING:

50 g (2 oz) candied and dried fruits
(sultanas, raisins, currants, candied peel, dried apricots) soaked
 overnight in 30 ml (2 tablespoons) Galliano liqueur
25 g (1 oz) pine kernels
350 g (12 oz) ricotta
3 large egg yolks
80 g (3 oz) caster sugar
grated zest of 1 lemon
25 g (1 oz) plain flour
150 ml (5 fl oz) double cream, whipped lightly

1   Use the cocoa pastry to line a deep 20 cm (8-inch) flan tin. Chill for 1 hour.

2   Preheat the oven to Gas Mark 5/electric oven 190°C/fan oven 170°C. Place a baking sheet on the middle shelf.

3   On the warmed baking sheet, bake the pastry case blind for 15 minutes. Remove the foil or paper and beans and return to the oven for a further 5 minutes.

4   Toast the pine kernels in the oven for 4–5 minutes until golden, watch them carefully as they burn easily! Reduce the temperature to Gas Mark 3/electric oven 160°C/fan oven 140°C.

5   Beat the ricotta until smooth. Whisk together the egg yolks, sugar and lemon zest until you have a thick and light mixture. Add the ricotta to the mixture and fold in the flour, followed by the whipped cream, fruit and nuts with any unabsorbed Galliano.

6   Spoon the filling into the cooked case and bake for 50 minutes, or until the filling is just set (it will carry on cooking for a little while after it comes out of the oven). This tart is best served chilled.

SERVES 6–8
PREPARATION & COOKING TIME:
30 minutes + 1 hour chilling + 30 minutes cooking
FREEZING: not suitable

FRENCH APPLE FLAN

This is one of my old favourites – I can still remember in my early student days spending many a Sunday afternoon perfecting this showpiece. It really does **look stunning** with its ever decreasing circles of red-rimmed apples, glistening under an apricot glaze – it never fails to please!

FOR THE PASTRY:
pâte sucrée made with 115 g (4 oz) flour (page 11)

FOR THE FILLING:
675 g (1½ lb) cooking apples, peeled, cored and sliced thinly
50 g (2 oz) granulated sugar
1 red eating apple
30 ml (2 tablespoons) lemon juice
2 tablespoons apricot jam, sieved and warmed

1   Line a 20 cm (8-inch) loose-bottomed, deep flan tin with the pâte sucrée. Chill for 1 hour.
2   Preheat the oven to Gas Mark 5/electric oven 190°C/fan oven 170°C. Place a baking tray in the middle of the oven.
3   On the warmed baking tray, bake the pastry case blind for 15 minutes. Remove the foil or paper and baking beans and cook for a further 5–10 minutes, until the pastry is fully cooked. Allow to cool.
4   In a medium saucepan, simmer the apples and sugar with 2 tablespoons water for 10–15 minutes until the apples are soft.
5   Pour the apple into a sieve and allow any excess liquid to drain off. Now push the apple mixture through the sieve to make a purée. Allow to cool.
6   Spoon the apple purée into the pastry case and level the surface.
7   Core and thinly slice the red apple. Arrange the slices in overlapping circles, starting from the edge. Brush the slices with lemon juice and then brush over the apricot jam to glaze.

I have so enjoyed writing this chapter, it seems that you can take your favourite sweet ingredients, set them in a flan case, and they cannot fail to look and taste wonderful. I have done this with rhubarb and custard, baking the rhubarb and topping it with a white chocolate crème pâtissière, sprinkled with a 'fleece' of chocolate shavings – see Rhubarb and White Chocolate Flan.

MODERN SWEET TARTS

Biscuit crumbs make simple, deliciously crunchy tart cases, and I have used this in Lemon and Lime Ginger Crunch Pie, and Rocky Road Ice Cream Pie. Fresh fruits in tarts taste gorgeous, barely cooked, but enough just to soften, and bring out their juices and flavour – see Plum Strudel Tartlets, and Pineapple Pastries. If you have a sweet tooth try the Banoffee Brandy Snap Tartlets – you won't be disappointed.

MAKES 6
PREPARATION TIME & COOKING TIME:
10 minutes + 5 minutes cooking
FREEZING: not recommended

Ready-made brandy snap baskets make ideal substitutes for the traditional ginger biscuit crumb base of Banoffee Pie and **they look so pretty** too. These tartlets need to be assembled shortly before eating, otherwise the baskets will soften – but all the preparation can be done in advance.

BANOFFEE BRANDY SNAP TARTLETS

80 g (3 oz) unsalted butter
80 g (3 oz) golden caster sugar
218 g can of condensed milk
100 g packet of 6 brandy snap baskets
2 small bananas, sliced and tossed in a little lemon juice
150 ml (5 fl oz) double cream, whipped lightly
15 g (½ oz) milk chocolate, grated

1 Melt the butter in a medium saucepan. Stir in the sugar and condensed milk. Bring this to the boil, stirring constantly. Cook over a medium heat for 5 minutes, stirring occasionally, until the sauce thickens slightly and becomes pale golden. Do not be tempted to cook for longer otherwise the mixture will separate.

2 Remove the pan from the heat and cover the surface of the banoffee mixture with a piece of wetted clingfilm. Leave to cool completely.

3 Spoon 1 tablespoon of banoffee mixture into each brandy snap case – you may have a spoonful left over.

4 Divide the banana between the baskets and spoon a dollop of cream on top.

5 Sprinkle with grated chocolate and serve immediately.

SERVES 10–12
PREPARATION & COOKING TIME:
30 minutes + 30 minutes chilling + 35–40 minutes cooking
FREEZING: recommended

DATE & APPLE STREUSEL PIE

Oats, breadcrumbs and toasted hazelnuts make a delectable light and crunchy topping for this tart. It cuts very well so makes **an ideal choice for a buffet**, being equally delicious hot or cold. Serve with a generous spoonful of West Country clotted cream.

FOR THE PASTRY:
shortcrust pastry made using 115 g (4 oz) flour (page 10)

FOR THE FILLING:
**115 g (4 oz) stoned dates,
chopped roughly
juice of 1 orange
40 g (1½ oz) caster sugar
1 tablespoon cornflour
550 g (1lb 4 oz) eating apples**

FOR THE STREUSEL TOPPING:
**50 g (2 oz) fresh wholemeal breadcrumbs
50 g (2 oz) rolled oats
50 g (2 oz) light muscovado sugar
25 g (1 oz) chopped roasted hazelnuts
50 g (2 oz) unsalted butter, melted**

1 Line a 23 cm (9-inch) loose-bottomed, deep flan tin with the shortcrust pastry and chill for 30 minutes.
2 Preheat the oven to Gas Mark 6/electric oven 200°C/fan oven 180°C. Place a baking sheet on the middle shelf of the oven.
3 Put the dates and orange juice in a small saucepan and simmer for about 5 minutes, until the juice has evaporated and the dates are soft. Allow to cool.
4 Combine the sugar and cornflour. Peel, core and thinly slice the apples. Stir the cornflour mixture into the sliced apples. Arrange a layer of apple over the pastry base. Now dot the date mixture on top and then cover with the remaining apple slices.
5 To make the streusel topping, stir the breadcrumbs, oats, sugar and hazelnuts into the butter. Scatter this over the apples.
6 Bake on the warmed baking sheet for 35–45 minutes, until the crumble is golden and the pastry is cooked – check the topping after 20–25 minutes, and cover with foil if it is sufficiently browned.

MAKES 12
PREPARATION & COOKING TIME: 25 minutes + 25 minutes baking
FREEZING: recommended

PLUM & MARZIPAN TARTS

I've used plums for this recipe but many other fruits, such as apricots, pears, apples and greengages, would work equally well. If you don't have the time to make almond paste, white marzipan can be rolled out and used instead. Do try making the paste if you can though – it really is very quick and easy and **the Amaretto gives it a lovely flavour**.

FOR THE PASTRY:
350 g (12 oz) ready-made puff pastry
I egg, beaten

FOR THE ALMOND PASTE:
115 g (4 oz) ground almonds
50 g (2 oz) caster sugar
50 g (2 oz) icing sugar
3–4 tablespoons Amaretto liqueur

FOR THE PLUM TOPPING:
900 g (2 lb) small plums, stoned and quartered
2 tablespoons redcurrant jelly, warmed, to glaze

1 Preheat the oven to Gas Mark 6/electric oven 200°C/fan oven 180°C.
2 Roll out the pastry on a lightly floured surface to make a rectangle 40 cm x 30 cm (16 inches x 12 inches). Cut it into 12 squares, each measuring 10 cm (4 inches). Place the squares on two baking sheets. Using a sharp knife, score a line 1 cm (½ inch) in from the edge around each one and prick the centres with a fork. Brush each square with beaten egg.
3 Combine the almond paste ingredients in a bowl, adding enough Amaretto to give a gritty sand-like texture. Spoon a tablespoon of paste on the centre of each pastry.
4 Arrange six pieces of plum, skin side up and overlapping, on each square within the scored border. Brush with redcurrant jelly.
5 Bake, one tray at a time, towards the top of the oven for 25 minutes, or until the pastries are puffy and golden. Remove them from the oven and brush once more with redcurrant jelly glaze.

SERVES 8
PREPARATION & COOKING TIME:
25 minutes + 20–25 minutes cooking
FREEZING: recommended

For me, this has to be one of the best fruit tart recipes – a combination of light puff pastry, soft almond cake and moist, concentrated fruits. Serve with clotted cream on a cold, wet, winter's day – **heaven**!

APRICOT, PRUNE & ORANGE MACAROON TART

FOR THE PASTRY:
350 g (12 oz) ready-made puff pastry

FOR THE FILLING:
150 g (5 oz) mixture of ready-soaked dried apricots and stoned prunes
grated zest and juice of ½ large orange
50 g (2 oz) unsalted butter, softened
50 g (2 oz) caster sugar
50 g (2 oz) ground almonds
1 large egg, beaten
50 g (2 oz) self-raising flour
¼ teaspoon baking powder
4–5 tablespoons no-added-sugar apricot spread or conserve
15 g (½ oz) flaked almonds
1 egg, beaten, to glaze
icing sugar, for dusting

1 Preheat the oven to Gas Mark 7/electric oven 220°C/fan oven 200°C.
2 Place the dried apricots and prunes in a small saucepan with the orange juice. Cover and simmer for about 20 minutes, or until all the liquid has evaporated.
3 To make the macaroon topping, cream the butter and sugar with the orange zest. Gradually beat in the ground almonds with the egg. Sift together the flour and baking powder and incorporate it into the macaroon mixture.
4 On a lightly floured surface roll out the pastry thinly. Find a large plate or round tray, 30 cm (12 inches) in diameter. Place it on the pastry and cut round it to make a circle. Place the circle on a baking sheet. Using a sharp knife, lightly score an inner circle, 4 cm (1½ inches) from the edge. Prick the pastry all over with a fork.

5 Spread a thin layer of apricot spread or conserve over the circle, as far as the marked line. Dot teaspoonfuls of macaroon mixture over the surface and lightly press the dried fruit into the pastry so that it fills the gaps.
6 Carefully turn the edges of the pastry in, as far as the scored line, to make a rim for the tart. Do this fairly tightly, folding over a couple of times, to make a tart approximately 23 cm (9 inches) in diameter. Scatter flaked almonds over the top and brush the pastry rim with beaten egg.
7 Bake in the centre of the oven for 20–25 minutes until the tart is risen and golden. Dust with sifted icing sugar and serve warm.

This would make a spectacular finale to any meal –

the shafts of transparent golden caramel resemble modern architectural sculptures as they rise above a smooth, creamy filling with a sharp fruity base. All the layers can be made in advance, but the tart needs to be assembled near to serving time as, after a few hours, the golden spires will start to dissolve back to their liquid state. If using frozen blackcurrants there is no need to add any water when cooking.

SERVES 8
PREPARATION & COOKING TIME:
25 minutes + 1 hour chilling
+ 25 minutes cooking
FREEZING: not recommended

BLACKCURRANT & CRACKED CARAMEL TART

FOR THE PASTRY:
pâte sucrée pastry made using
115 g (4 oz) plain flour (page 11)

FOR THE FILLING:
350 g (12 oz) blackcurrants
50 g (2 oz) light muscovado sugar
200 g tub of plain Greek yogurt
150 ml (5 fl oz) double cream
¼ teaspoon vanilla extract

FOR THE CARAMEL:
80 g (3 oz) granulated sugar
80 ml (3 fl oz) water

1 Line a 20 cm (8-inch) loose-bottomed, deep flan tin with the pâte sucrée. Chill for 1 hour.
2 Preheat the oven to Gas Mark 5/electric oven 190°C/fan oven 170°C. Place a baking sheet in the centre of the oven.
3 On the warmed baking sheet, bake the pastry case blind for 15 minutes. Remove the foil or paper and beans and continue cooking for a further 5–10 minutes, until the pastry is cooked through and golden in colour.
4 Gently heat the blackcurrants in a medium saucepan with the muscovado sugar and 2 tablespoons water for about 5 minutes, or until the fruit just softens, and the juices start to run. Cool and strain.
5 For the caramel, place the granulated sugar in a small saucepan with the water. Gently heat to dissolve the sugar.

Increase the heat and boil rapidly for about 15 minutes, until the syrup turns to a golden caramel. Pour it out on to a small baking tin lined with baking parchment. Cool until the caramel becomes brittle.
6 Place the yogurt, cream and vanilla extract in a bowl and beat gently until the mixture is smooth and just able to hold its shape.
7 Spoon the blackcurrants over the pastry base. Cover with the yogurt and cream filling. Break up the caramel roughly into jagged triangular shapes and arrange at various angles over the surface of the tart.

SERVES 6
PREPARATION & COOKING TIME:
25 minutes + 1 hour chilling
+ 20–25 minutes cooking
FREEZING: not recommended

'Truly scrumptious' is probably a fair description of this tart. It looks stunning, is simple to make and tastes divine! It epitomizes summer dining – light, yet rich in flavour. **The colours in this tart are really vibrant.**

FOR THE PASTRY:
sweet rich shortcrust pastry made with 115 g (4 oz) flour (page 10)

FOR THE FILLING:
150 g (5 oz) white chocolate (the drops are good for this)
250 g tub of mascarpone
200 g tub of plain fromage frais
¼ teaspoon vanilla extract
225 g (8 oz) fresh raspberries
1½ tablespoons redcurrant jelly

1 Line a 23 cm (9-inch) loose-bottomed, shallow flan tin with the pastry. Chill for 1 hour.
2 Preheat the oven to Gas Mark 5/electric oven 190°C/fan oven 170°C. Place a baking tray in the centre of the oven.
3 On the heated baking sheet, bake the pastry case for 15 minutes. Remove the foil or paper and beans and continue cooking for a further 5–10 minutes, until the pastry is cooked through.
4 Melt the chocolate in a bowl over a pan of barely simmering water.
5 Meanwhile, beat together the mascarpone, fromage frais and vanilla, until smooth. Stir in the melted chocolate. Spoon the mixture into the pastry case. Level the surface.
6 Scatter the raspberries over the top and brush with warmed redcurrant jelly.

RASPBERRY, WHITE CHOCOLATE & VANILLA TART

SERVES 8
PREPARATION & COOKING TIME:
25 minutes + 1 hour chilling
+ 50 minutes cooking
FREEZING: not recommended

This custard is to die for! It has such a **melt-in-the-mouth** texture. It is almost an upside-down crème caramel with caramel being poured over the gooseberries and the custard on top. I could only find frozen gooseberries and they worked perfectly – do not be alarmed by the amount of liquid they produce, it all reduces to a caramel, I promise.

GOOSEBERRY FLAN WITH ELDERFLOWER CUSTARD

FOR THE PASTRY:
pâte sucrée made using 115 g (4 oz) flour (page 11)

FOR THE FILLING:
80 g (3 oz) unsalted butter
50 g (2 oz) granulated sugar
450 g (1 lb) fresh or frozen gooseberries, topped and tailed
2 large eggs plus 2 large yolks
25 g (1 oz) caster sugar
300 ml (10 fl oz) double cream
2 tablespoons elderflower cordial

1 Line a 20 cm (8-inch) loose-bottomed, deep flan tin with the pâte sucrée. Chill for 1 hour.
2 Preheat the oven to Gas Mark 5/electric oven 190°C/fan oven 170°C. Place a baking tray in the middle of the oven.
3 On the warmed baking tray, bake the pastry case blind for 15 minutes. Remove the foil or paper and beans and continue cooking for a further 5–10 minutes.
4 Melt the butter in a medium saucepan and stir in the granulated sugar. Stir until the sugar is dissolved and then add the gooseberries. Simmer for about 10 minutes, until the fruit is just tender.

5 Using a slotted spoon remove the gooseberries. Turn the heat up and boil rapidly until the liquid has reduced and caramelised. Spoon the gooseberries into the pastry case and pour over the caramel.
6 Beat together the eggs, yolks, caster sugar, cream and elderflower cordial. Pour this over the gooseberries. Bake for about 30 minutes, or until just set. Leave to cool slightly and serve warm.

SERVES 8
PREPARATION & COOKING TIME:
10 minutes + 30 minutes chilling
+ 3–5 minutes cooking
FREEZING: essential

Susie and James, our two eldest children, thought that this was **'the best'**, and would have awarded it an **A*** if the biscuit base was replaced with just Maltesers – they do give it a lovely surprise crunch. This 'pile it high' ice cream pie would make a great special-occasion pudding for kids.

ROCKY ROAD ICE CREAM PIE

80 g (3 oz) unsalted butter
200 g (7 oz) chocolate digestive biscuits
500 ml tub of good quality toffee ice cream, softened slightly
58 g (giant size!) bag of Maltesers – halved if you can!
2 large egg whites
115 g (4 oz) caster sugar
50 g (2 oz) coloured mini marshmallows

1 Preheat the oven to Gas Mark 8/electric oven 230°C/fan oven 210°C.
2 Melt the butter in a medium saucepan. Crush the digestive biscuits and stir them into the butter. Press the crumb mixture into the base and sides of a buttered 20 cm (8-inch) loose-bottomed, deep flan tin. Chill for 30 minutes.
3 Scoop half the ice cream out and pack it carefully into the biscuit case. Press half the Maltesers randomly on top. Repeat this with the remaining ice cream and Maltesers.

4 Whisk the egg whites until stiff. Gradually beat in half the sugar. Fold in the rest, reserving 1 teaspoon and then add the marshmallows. Spread this meringue mixture completely over the ice cream and Maltesers, leaving nothing visible underneath. Make dramatic swirls with the meringue and sprinkle with the reserved sugar.
5 Bake as near the top of the oven as possible for 3–5 minutes, watching carefully, until the meringue is just crisp and browned. Serve at once.

SERVES 8
PREPARATION & COOKING TIME:
15 minutes + 30 minutes chilling
FREEZING: not recommended

LEMON & LIME GINGER CRUNCH PIE

This recipe is based on one of those classic dishes of the 70s. Its **ease of preparation** and few, mainly store cupboard, ingredients still make it an attractive dessert today. It requires virtually no cooking and is best left to chill overnight, but will set within an hour if need be.

FOR THE BISCUIT BASE:
80 g (3 oz) unsalted butter
175 g (6 oz) ginger nut biscuits

FOR THE FILLING:
grated zest and juice of 2 limes,
grated zest and juice of 2 lemons
397 g can of sweetened condensed milk
300 ml (10 fl oz) double cream
grated chocolate, to decorate

1   Melt the butter in a medium saucepan over a low heat. Meanwhile put the ginger nuts in a polythene bag and crush them with a rolling pin to a sand-like consistency.
2   Stir the crumbs into the butter. Press the crumb mixture into the base and up the sides of a 20 cm (8-inch) ceramic flan dish. Chill for at least 30 minutes.
3   Put all the filling ingredients into a mixing bowl. Whisk for about 2 minutes until the mixture is thick and creamy. Pour this into the crumb case and chill overnight until set. Decorate with a sprinkling of grated chocolate.

MAKES 6
PREPARATION & COOKING TIME:
10 minutes + 15–20 minutes cooking
FREEZING: recommended

PINEAPPLE PASTRIES

Pineapple topped with sugary spice makes a perfect partner for pastry because of its **intense flavour**. Make sure that your pineapple is ripe and juicy, otherwise use the canned variety – you can also buy very good ready-prepared fresh pineapple in most supermarkets. It is so quick to make you will not believe how such a simple recipe can taste so good. Serve warm with pouring cream.

FOR THE PASTRY:
350 g (12 oz) ready-made puff pastry
1 egg, beaten
1 tablespoon icing sugar

FOR THE FILLING:
½ small fresh pineapple, approximately
**   350 g (12 oz) unprepared weight**
25 g (1 oz) unsalted butter, melted
2 tablespoons demerara sugar
1 teaspoon mixed spice

1   Preheat the oven to Gas Mark 7/electric oven 220°C/ fan oven 200°C.
2   On a lightly floured surface roll out the pastry thinly. Use a 10 cm (4-inch) diameter round guide to cut out six circles. Place the circles on a baking tray. Using a sharp knife, Score a line 1 cm (½ inch) in from the edge of each circle. Prick the pastry well with a fork.
3   Brush the pastry all over with the beaten egg and dredge with icing sugar.
4   Remove the skin and core from the pineapple. Slice it fairly thinly and cut into triangles. Divide these triangles between the pastries, taking care to keep the fruit within the inner circle.
5   Brush the pineapple with melted butter. Mix together the sugar and mixed spice and sprinkle this liberally all over the pastries.
6   Bake towards the top of the oven for 15–20 minutes, until the pastries are crisp and golden and the pineapple is beginning to caramelise.

SERVES 6
PREPARATION & COOKING TIME:
20 minutes + 30 minutes chilling
+ 25 minutes cooking
FREEZING: not recommended

This crunchy pastry is almost good enough to make into biscuits! A wonderfully fragrant autumn or winter tart for when there is little other fruit around. Ginger gives a subtle warming undertone to the distinctive cardamom flavour. Serve this **comforting pudding** with a dollop of crème fraîche or vanilla ice cream.

FOR THE ORANGE AND OATMEAL PASTRY:

80 g (3 oz) plain flour
25 g (1 oz) medium oatmeal
50 g (2 oz) caster sugar
grated zest of 1 orange
80 g (3 oz) unsalted butter, diced
1 tablespoon freshly squeezed orange juice

FOR THE TOPPING:

25 g (1 oz) unsalted butter
50 g (2 oz) caster sugar
7 medium bananas
¼ teaspoon ground ginger
seeds of 10 cardamom pods, crushed (about ¼ teaspoon)

1 To make the pastry, mix together the flour, oatmeal, sugar and orange zest. Rub in the butter and bind it all to a dough with the orange juice. Bring it together to form a ball and wrap it in a polythene bag. Chill for at least 30 minutes.
2 Preheat the oven to Gas Mark 6/electric oven 200°C/fan oven 180°C. Place a baking sheet on the middle shelf of the oven.
3 Prepare the topping by warming a 23 cm (9-inch) skillet over a medium heat. Melt the butter and then sprinkle caster sugar evenly over the surface. Cook for 1–2 minutes, until you see it just beginning to caramelise. Remove the pan from the heat. Take care with this as the mixture will continue to cook and darken further, even when it is removed from the heat.
4 Peel the bananas and cut them into five batons. Arrange them to cover the base of the skillet, packing them closely together.
5 Sprinkle ground ginger and cardamom over the bananas.
6 On a lightly floured surface roll out the pastry to a 24 cm (9½-inch) round. Using the rolling pin to help you, place the pastry over the bananas, and tuck in any spare down the edges.
7 On the warmed baking sheet, bake at once for about 25 minutes, or until the pastry is crisp and golden. Remove from the oven and allow it to stand for about 10 minutes before inverting it on to a serving plate. This tart is best eaten warm.

NOTE: If you don't own a skillet use a heavy-based saucepan for step 3, and then pour the caramel into a 23 cm (9-inch) shallow, round cake tin. Arrange the bananas on top.

SPICED CARAMELISED BANANAS WITH ORANGE & OATMEAL CRUST

SERVES 8
PREPARATION & COOKING TIME:
25 minutes + 30 minutes chilling
+ 40 minutes cooking
FREEZING: not recommended

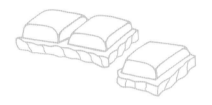

This is one of my **favourite tart recipes** – a complete pudding in itself, without the need for any accompaniments! A thick covering of white chocolate shavings gives a feathery effect to the dessert. You will need to assemble this flan just a couple of hours before serving, as the rhubarb does tend to make the pastry shell go soggy.

FOR THE RHUBARB FILLING:
**450 g (1 lb) trimmed rhubarb, cut into
2.5 cm (1-inch) batons
50 g (2 oz) golden caster sugar**

FOR THE PASTRY:
**sweet rich shortcrust pastry made
with 115 g (4 oz) flour (page 10)**

FOR THE CRÈME PÂTISSIÈRE:
**2 large eggs
50 g (2 oz) caster sugar
1 rounded tablespoon plain flour
1 rounded tablespoon cornflour
300 ml (10 fl oz) milk
¼ teaspoon vanilla extract
150 g (5 oz) white chocolate**

1   Line a 20 cm (8-inch) loose-bottomed, deep flan tin with the pastry. Chill for 30 minutes.
2   Preheat the oven to Gas Mark 5/electric oven 90°C/fan oven 170°C. Place a baking tray on the middle shelf of the oven.
3   Place the rhubarb in a shallow baking dish and sprinkle with the sugar. Bake in the oven for 30–40 minutes, stirring a couple of times during cooking. Remove from the oven and cool.
4   For the crème pâtissière, whisk together the eggs and sugar, until thick and creamy. Sift together flour and cornflour and add this to the egg mixture. Heat the milk in a medium saucepan to just below boiling point and pour this on to the egg mixture, stirring continuously. Return it all to the pan and bring slowly to a simmer. Simmer for 1 minute, stirring all the time. Stir in the vanilla.
5   Melt 80 g (3 oz) of the white chocolate in a bowl over a pan of hot (not boiling) water. Beat the chocolate into the crème pâtissière. Pour it into a bowl to cool and press some dampened clingfilm on to the surface to prevent a skin from forming.
6   On the warmed baking tray, bake the pastry shell blind for 15 minutes. Remove the foil and beans and return it to the oven for a further 5 minutes until the pastry is crisp and golden. Allow to cool.
7   When you are ready to assemble the flan, carefully ease the pastry case from the tin. Strain any juices off the rhubarb and scatter the fruit over the base of the flan. Smooth the white chocolate crème pâtissière over the top. Grate the remaining chocolate and sprinkle it all over the flan.

RHUBARB & WHITE CHOCOLATE FLAN

MAKES 12
PREPARATION & COOKING TIME:
20 minutes + 50–55 minutes cooking
FREEZING: recommended

While I was developing this recipe our decorator was busy wallpapering the next door room, and I couldn't help but be drawn by the similarities of our tasks when it comes to measuring up filo pastry! Both end results, I'm glad to say, were very satisfactory, although the result of the decorator's endeavours has stayed around for considerably longer than mine! **Serve these hot or warm** accompanied by crème fraîche.

FOR THE PASTRY:
**2 x 48 cm x 26 cm (19 inch x 10 inch)
sheets filo pastry
25 g (1 oz) butter, melted**

FOR THE FILLING:
**350 g (12 oz) small plums, halved and stoned
25 g (1 oz) caster sugar
4 trifle sponges
2 tablespoons Amaretto
25 g (1 oz) ratafia or amaretti biscuits
15 g (½ oz) flaked almonds**

1   Preheat the oven to Gas Mark 4/electric oven 180°C/fan oven 160°C.
2   Place the plums in a shallow baking dish with 2 tablespoons cold water and sprinkle over the sugar. Bake them for 35–40 minutes until tender, spoon over the juices half way through the cooking time.
3   For the filo tartlets, lay out the sheets of filo on the work surface, on top of each other with edges matching. Arrange the pastry so that the shortest edge is at the top. Cut it from top to bottom into three equal strips. Now cut across the centre of each strip. You should have six pieces. Stack these on top of each other and cut across them twice to make squares.
4   Take a 12-hole patty tin. Brush each square generously with butter. Lay three squares, at an angle, in each hole so that you have a sort of star effect. Fill all 12 holes in this way.
5   Break up the trifle sponges and place them in the pastry tarts – one sponge per three pastry cases. Sprinkle Amaretto over the sponge so that it soaks up the flavour.
6   Remove the plums from the oven and allow them to cool slightly. Increase the temperature to Gas Mark 5/electric oven 190°C/fan oven 170°C. Cut the plums into bite-size pieces. Place three plum pieces in each tart. Spoon 1 teaspoon of plum juice over each.
7   Place the ratafia or amaretti biscuits in a polythene bag and crush them with a rolling pin. Mix the flaked almonds into the crumbs. Scatter this strudel topping over the tartlets.
8   Bake in the centre of the oven for approximately 15 minutes until the pastry and toppings are golden.

PLUM STRUDEL TARTLETS

This is a wonderful summertime flan that can be made the night before and assembled on the day. You can substitute peaches for the nectarines. Fresh raspberries would go well in place of the blueberries – but do not bake them. Walnut pastry sounds difficult to make, but it is not at all, and if you omit the sugar it would be ideal for use in any savoury flan.

SERVES 8
PREPARATION & COOKING TIME:
30 minutes + 1 hour chilling
+ 30–35 minutes cooking
FREEZING: not recommended

BAKED NECTARINE & BLUEBERRY TART

FOR THE WALNUT PASTRY:
50 g (2 oz) unsalted butter
115 g (4 oz) plain flour
25 g (1 oz) walnuts, ground
2 tablespoons caster sugar
1 large egg yolk

FOR THE FILLING:
3 ripe nectarines
juice of 1 lemon
115 g (4 oz) blueberries
50 g (2 oz) caster sugar
250 g tub of mascarpone
150 ml (5 fl oz) double cream
¼ teaspoon vanilla essence
2 tablespoons icing sugar

1 First of all make the walnut pastry. Rub the butter into the flour until the mixture resembles fine breadcrumbs. Stir in the ground walnuts and sugar. Add the egg yolk and 1 tablespoon cold water. Bring it all together to form a smooth dough.

2 Roll out the dough on a lightly floured surface. Use it to line a 20 cm (8-inch) round, loose-bottomed, deep flan tin. Prick the base all over with a fork, cover, and chill for about 1 hour.

3 Preheat the oven to Gas Mark 5/electric oven 190°C/fan oven 170°C.

4 Cut the nectarines into quarters and discard the stones. Place them in a non-metallic baking dish and sprinkle with lemon juice. Spoon the sugar evenly over the fruit and bake towards the top of the oven for 20 minutes. Now stir the nectarines to coat them with the juices,

and sprinkle the blueberries over the top. Return to the oven for a further 5 minutes, until the nectarines are tinged golden. Remove from the oven and allow to cool.

5 Increase the oven temperature to Gas Mark 6/electric oven 200°C/fan oven 180°C and put a baking sheet on the middle shelf. On the warmed baking sheet, bake the pastry case blind for 15 minutes. Remove the foil and beans and cook for a further 5–10 minutes until crisp and golden. Leave to cool.

6 When you are ready to assemble the tart whisk together mascarpone, cream, vanilla and sugar until you have a thick and smooth mixture. Spread this over the base of the pastry shell. Pile the baked fruits on top and spoon over any juices just prior to serving.

SERVES 8
PREPARATION & COOKING TIME:
25 minutes + 1 hour chilling
+ 45–50 minutes baking
FREEZING: not recommended

The combination of chocolate and hazelnuts never fails to please, and ground almonds could be substituted if you prefer. This chocolate tart has a **lovely, light mousse-like texture** and is delicious served with crème fraîche, which has been sweetened and flavoured with Cointreau. If you find the pastry difficult to handle – it can be a little crumbly – press it into the tin, rather than rolling it out.

WARM CHOCOLATE TART

FOR THE HAZELNUT PASTRY:
115 g (4 oz) plain flour
25 g (1 oz) roasted chopped hazelnuts, ground
50 g (2 oz) unsalted butter, diced
25 g (1 oz) caster sugar
1 egg, beaten

FOR THE FILLING:
115 g (4 oz) dark chocolate with minimum 70% cocoa solids, broken into pieces
25 g (1 oz) unsalted butter
2 large eggs
50 g (2 oz) golden caster sugar
150 ml (5 fl oz) double cream
icing sugar, for dusting

1 Combine the flour and ground hazelnuts in a bowl. Rub in the butter until the mixture resembles breadcrumbs. Stir in the sugar. Add enough egg to make a soft dough. Roll out the dough on a lightly floured surface, and use it to line a greased 20 cm (8-inch) loose-bottomed, deep flan ring. Prick the base with a fork and chill for 1 hour.

2 Preheat the oven to Gas Mark 5/electric oven 190°C/fan oven 170°C. Place a baking sheet in the centre of the oven.

3 On the warmed baking sheet, bake the pastry case blind for 15 minutes. Remove the foil or paper and baking beans and cook for a further 5–10 minutes. Reduce the oven temperature to Gas Mark 4/electric oven 180°C/fan oven 160°C.

4 Melt the chocolate and butter in a bowl over hot (not boiling) water. Stir until smooth and then leave to cool slightly.

5 Whisk the eggs and sugar together, until thick and pale, this will take about 5 minutes. Fold in the chocolate mixture followed by the double cream. Pour this into the flan case and bake for about 20 minutes. The tart should still have a slight tremble in the centre, and will continue to cook when it is removed from the oven.

6 When ready to serve, remove the tart carefully from the flan tin, dust with sifted icing sugar and serve warm.

SERVES 8
PREPARATION & COOKING TIME:
25 minutes + 30 minutes chilling + 15 minutes cooking
FREEZING: not recommended

MOCHA PIE WITH BAILEYS

This pie is really rich and has a lovely fudgy texture. A combination of layers – a biscuit base, a coffee centre flavoured with Baileys and a smooth chocolate cream top – ensures a mix of **wonderful flavours and textures**. It is equally delicious warm or cold.

FOR THE BASE:
200 g (7 oz) digestive biscuits, crushed
80 g (3 oz) unsalted butter, melted

FOR THE FILLING:
80 g (3 oz) unsalted butter, softened
80 g (3 oz) light muscovado sugar
1 large egg + 1 large yolk
2 tablespoons self-raising flour
2 tablespoons instant coffee dissolved in 1 tablespoon boiling water
1 tablespoon Baileys liqueur

FOR THE TOPPING:
80 g (3 oz) milk chocolate
3 tablespoons double cream

1 Preheat the oven to Gas Mark 5/electric oven 190°C/fan oven 170°C.
2 Combine the crushed biscuits and melted butter. Press the crumb mixture into the base, and up the sides of a 20 cm (8-inch) loose-bottomed, shallow flan tin. Chill for at least 30 minutes.
3 Cream together the butter and sugar until pale. Separate the whole egg. Gradually beat in the yolks. Fold in the flour, followed by the coffee and Baileys. Whisk the egg white until stiff and fold it in (don't worry if the mixture curdles). Pour this into the crumb case and bake in the oven for 15 minutes, or until the filling is just set.
4 Melt the chocolate and cream in a bowl over a pan of hot, not boiling, water. Stir until smooth and pour this over the tart while it is still warm. Spread it evenly over the surface.